A Spiritual Journey

Volume I

By Morgan Louise Russell

Copyright © 2021 by Morgan Louise Russell
ISBN 9781737881216

For all of the students. We are all Fools, led by the adventure of infinite potential.

♡ Cover art by Eva Miller who herself is art in human form ♡

Connect with or find more creations by Eva via Instagram, @whodrewit

♡ Chapter 1 ♡

Like My Appetite, My Curiosity is Insatiable!

I wrote all of my experiences down.

In a scattered, haphazard way. But I did it nonetheless and, because I love a story with great parallels and connections, I felt compelled to organize them. This work is the result. A chronology from the very beginning, onward. A journey of expansion that hasn't reached finality. I don't suspect there will ever be a conclusion. On the contrary, you can expect a conclusion at the end of this volume. I've found that I'm decently skilled at creating comprehensive, tied-together partings. I'm not very skilled in the area of beginning or, rather, knowing where to start, but since it's imperative, an introduction must be attempted.

Picture me, your typical chaotic-good girl-next-door, with grades worthy of grandma's fridge and a group of eclectic friends that weren't so eclectic that it wasn't normal. Normal. That's the key word that characterized my life; that which I connected to with ease. I grew up in a small town in a typical middle-class manner, with two hard working parents, a protective older brother, and a lazy, yellow labrador named Scooby-Doo. My middle name came from three grandma's; three strong women before me. I was gifted the notorious, but only slight, Russell overbite from my dad and thick hair from my momma. I worked hard in school; even harder in sports. I pushed my curfew later as I grew, to make sure I had time for spray-painting train cars and playing hide and seek with pals throughout town. I did all of the things that made me normal. Like getting a job at my best friend's family bakery when I turned 16, washing dishes and dipping cake pops in melted chocolate. Fighting with my big brother, who I think had the bigger attitude but he disagrees. Day-dreaming of the future, while doing my best to stay present.

I was raised to be kind, by even kinder parents. And raised to be curious, by the curious "reality" we live in. A "reality" that, I found, is more questionable by the day.

My first experience of the curiosity of this "reality" was seeing shadows silently walk into my bedroom. The second experience was noticing the similarities that arose between my everyday life and the "scary" stories that weren't supposed to be real. But the pivotal moment was when my momma let me in on the secret that nothing is really as it seems. And from that point on, like my appetite, my curiosity has been insatiable.

As casually as could be, I began my spiritual journey in a small town in northeastern Wisconsin. It's been a rollercoaster of developing psychic, mediumistic, and healing abilities that run in the family, tackling my pesky human ego and fluctuating energy, and surrendering to the journey that unfolds before me. With curiosity leading the way, I stepped into my lifelong role as a student.

And I wrote all of my experiences down.

♡ Chapter 2 ♡

You Don't Get Labeled a Witch By Being Average!

It seems the best approach if I provide a rundown of where it all began, in order to understand where the journey is going in a linear sense.

My experiences began many years ago. Before I ever held my crush's hand, drove a car, or had a really bad hangover. I was barely subjected to the very physical world around me when these paranormal experiences and unorthodox curiosities happened upon me. One unsuspecting day, my momma threw a curveball my way. This henceforth was my indoctrination into the spiritual.

The year is 2008. Or somewhere around that time. The point is, I was that innocent and naive kiddo mentioned a moment ago. I had tagged along with my momma rummage-saling one early morning, where we both hoped to score neat finds. My momma, *another* set of antique dishes that would sit in storage. Me, a book that I would add to my future library. But rather than chipped china plates or Christmas-themed drinking glasses, my momma took a liking to a very old, black mirror.

"It's used for divination in witchcraft," my momma explained, wiggling her eyebrows at me.

At the time, this meant very little to me. But my puny brain did register "witchcraft". Naturally, I did what kids do, and I used my limited life experiences to form a quick and ridiculous conclusion.

Holy crap, my momma's a witch.

The Hollywood-ized kind. The kind that flies around on a broom, cackling at the moon. The kind that creates her reality with the use of potions and spells. I'm talking about the cauldron-brewing, wand-wielding, massive boil-on-her-nose kind of witch.

After this monumental and uncomfortable epiphany overcame me, I was intimidated by my momma. I'm sure you can imagine how on edge I was when she opened up to my brother and I about her "abilities" shortly thereafter. But we soon realized these abilities weren't characterized by enchantments or incantations. At least not in the way Hollywood led us to believe.

"Spirits are real, and I can communicate with them. And I can heal people and animals with my hands. Oh, and I'm also psychic."

These weren't my momma's exact, eloquent words, but rather the short, to the point version of what that conversation entailed. Spirits are real? But society had been trying to convince us otherwise since birth. What a bold move to share that message with your nine and eleven-year-old kids, Michelle. Healing hands? We must protect my momma at all costs, so the government doesn't find out. And psychic? For the first couple of days I kept my thoughts closely in check, worried that I would internally rat on myself for forgetting to let Scooby out or for drinking three Dr. Peppers in a row. But shortly after I realized I was in the clear. It wasn't so black and white.

Flash forward a few years and here we are. My momma, communicating with spirits, offering messages to those who need them, and making the world a better place by the patience she practices and the love she so willingly gives. And me, asking my momma an endless amount of questions to prove that I'm not crazy, while absorbing everything I can from her lessons, the unique experiences that I've been privy to over the years, and of course, the Universe that never quits.

This illusion we call life is funny sometimes; the parallels that occur. A few years ago I was convinced my momma was a witch. Today, people in our community have claimed my momma and I to be the same kind of Hollywood-ized witches. It always makes me giggle when I think of it. That's when I knew we were on the brink of something great. You don't get labeled a witch by being average.

I was young when my momma embraced her abilities, so I didn't initially grasp the full extent of what she would attempt to explain to me. But man, was I open-minded and receptive to what my little brain could comprehend. Aside from simply being young and naive, it was difficult to question my momma. My momma, who was *always* right, and *always* genuine. Through the years, my momma has radiated warmth, truth, and unconditional love. Anyone who has had the pleasure of meeting her can testify. She is full of wisdom and goodness, and a whole grocery list of other positive characteristics. That is precisely why she has been given the abilities she has. I believed her and every recount she told me. Skepticism be damned! But there came a time when I no longer had to take her word for the strange and unbelievable things she experienced. I didn't have to settle for believing her anymore because I began to open up to all of the "crazy" and "impossible".

*   *   *   *   *

Now way, way back when I was just a lil peanut, I experienced the first phenomena that came with the abilities I was given. This was even before my momma came out of the spiritual closet; before she embraced the natural pull towards her spiritual abilities. That phenomenon was being visited by spirits at all hours of the night. And as a young child, I didn't know what to make of this. Parents and guardians, I see the appeal in passing these experiences off as nightmares or shadows or too much candy before bed. Trust me, I would have *loved* to hear this if I *actually* believed it in the slightest. But I didn't.

"There's no one here, you were just having a nightmare. Ghosts aren't real!"

Those attempts at talking down the experience don't usually diminish the authenticity of the experience. I would wake in the middle of the night more often than not with people standing in my doorway, at the foot of my bed, or walking towards me. And let me tell you, even as a 5-10 year old, I felt pretty crazy hearing from my parents that nothing was there when I was more certain about the fact that there was something there than I was about the Earth being round. It was just my imagination. What an *astounding* imagination I had then. I should write *books!*

It first began back on Armstrong Street, the house I grew up in from my debut days on Earth in this lifetime to probably nine years old. I remember more than once in my foggy early memories waking up to see someone standing in my bedroom. One specific time, a figure walked from the dark hallway into my even darker bedroom to stand at the foot of my bed.

"Dad?" I questioned the tall figure, hoping for the best.

There was no answer, so naturally I screamed. I screamed my little six-year-old lungs off.

Fast-forward a few years. We packed our lives up in boxes and toted them all out to the country. Edwards Avenue was our new domain, and still the late night entertainment continued. They stepped up their game, strategizing on how to more effectively give little Morgan the creeps, or so it seemed to me. One night, after falling asleep in my hip and brand new nine-year-old bedroom, fresh with blue-striped walls that my dad lovingly painted at my request, I woke up to a scene that still freaks me out to think of. There were three figures standing at the end of my bed, their bodies illuminated by the light coming from the hallway. They stood next to each other, lined up from tallest to shortest, all waving at me. The only thing that would have been more terrifying in hindsight would be switching the vague figures out for old-timey children. My two bugaboos: dolls and creepy, old-timey children.

  I threw the covers over my head; the most effective tool in protecting me from the intruders. Like usual, I screamed bloody murder and waited for my parents to reach my upstairs bedroom. I can still hear the sound of them racing up the stairs, including the specific creaks of the steps, from the multitude of times that I flipped the crap out.

  And if you thought I only had these experiences in the comfort of my own home, you thought wrong. Spirits followed everywhere. One summer I was invited by my friend to go camping for the weekend with her family. We stayed in a tricked-out camper, on the bottom half of a bunk-bed shared by her brother. I was on the outside of the bed, and woke up in the middle of the night to see two figures standing next to the bed. One was tall, one was short. They were so close to me I could have poked them. But I didn't do that. Instead, I chose to scream. And my scream of choice was, "MOMMMMMMMMMMMMMMM!".

  As you can imagine, I was teased by everyone the next day. If I had been any older, I probably would have been mortified. But not nine-year-old Morgan. She was prepubescent, and had no shame.

  I'm sure I nearly put my momma and dad into cardiac arrest more than once from my terrified screams in the middle of the night. In the years following, I screamed less. But when I'd wake in the night to see something, the fight-or-flight instincts would still kick in. I was more combative at this point. Instead of hiding under the covers and screaming the spirits away, I would race down the stairs all the way to my parent's bedroom with a pillow and blanket in hand. But eventually, even though I still saw things more often than not in the night, I would stick it out. I was embarrassed by the fact that I had to find comfort on the floor of my parent's bedroom. Especially with the idea being reinforced constantly that *there was nothing there*. I would do whatever it took to stay up in my room. Most of the time I could get by with just keeping my TV on all night. My dad would get so frustrated to find that it was still on in the morning. Every night when he'd come up and say goodnight he'd make me set a sleep timer, but I'd always turn it off when he left the room. I'm sure he caught on. Other times I would shut my door and try to sleep with my light on all night. There were even times that I would just try to stay awake as long as I could, before I got so tired that I couldn't fight the sleepiness. With that option, I would sleep straight until I had to wake up for school the next morning. No run-ins with things that went bump in the night. In addition to those tactics, I'd say a quick prayer, which was more like me begging whoever was listening to give me peace until morning. Sometimes it worked, sometimes it didn't. But I had survived thus far, and I'd be damned if I was giving up that easily.

Mystical experiences have been a part of my life for as long as I can remember, but at varying degrees throughout the years. Looking back, it's evident that I've always been a little weirdo. I've just managed to hide it well. I've always been shamelessly attracted to the spooky, the bizarre, the unknown. That's why I had a ghost in the graveyard birthday party at a funeral home when I turned twelve. We had connections. I think back on that now and realize how crass that must have seemed. Or why after going to the movies and seeing a horror film, I'd deem it necessary that our carload of friends go sneak out to the country and explore the abandoned and decrepit house hidden in the woods. Or why it was more likely to find me watching a SYFY movie than cartoons on a Saturday morning. I used to live for *Jeepers Creepers*.

Being curious about the spooky, hard-to-explain things in life led me to explore hobbies like hypnosis. I'd go over to my friends' houses with a necklace and attempt to hypnotize them. As you'd likely imagine, it never worked.

"You have to *believe* that it'll work. Don't treat it like it's a joke! It's not funny. This is real!" I would explain. But try as I might, it still didn't work. It turns out most people need adequate training to be able to hypnotize others. You don't just magically become Dr. Brian Weiss by waving a friendship necklace in front of some kid hyped up on sugar at a slumber party.

Throughout middle school when we were forced to do future career questionnaires to discover our passions, people were lumped into the categories of doctors, performers, engineers, etc. And I wanted to be a hypnotherapist, specializing in past-life regression. But I couldn't tell that to my guidance counselor. She had already rejected my best friend's dream of becoming a baker. Jokes on me, because those questionnaires were intended to prevent indecision, and here I am - a broke college student who wants to do everything. Study everything. Know everything. The indecision is real.

"You have time to figure it out," they say.

But I only blinked and my undergrad has reached finality.

Another hobby that I picked up voraciously and still carry with me today is watching scary movies. My obsessive behavior with horror films began when my aunt and uncle let my brother and I pick out the movie-night movie for our slumber party back around the mid-2000s.

"*The Amityville Horror*," we declared, flipping through their expansive collection of burned DVD's.

"That's a really scary movie, are you sure you can handle it?" they asked.

ArE yOu SuRe YoU cAn HaNdLe It?

But roughly fourteen years later and I'm still scared of closets. Especially when my brother pushes me in and stands in front of the door so I can't get out. Tanner must have been my brother in previous lifetimes. He plays the part in this lifetime all too well. If you don't know what I'm referring to with the closet, do yourself a favor and watch the movie. Any chance at a normal life venturing in and out of small rooms dedicated to coats and brooms was corrupted by that film. Thanks a lot, Ryan Reynolds. But as a result, I developed an affinity for all things scary in the years to come. You could say this was my indoctrination into the spooky.

When I was around 10 years old, my dad lived in one city while my momma lived in another thirty minutes away. That's called divorce. When staying with my momma, we commuted those thirty minutes to school everyday. But she had a Yukon with a DVD player in it, so it was chill and there were few complaints. Every morning on our drive to school, my brother and I would watch either *The Texas Chainsaw Massacre* or *Freddy vs. Jason*. Both classics, in my opinion. Comparable to the likes of *Titanic, Gone with the Wind,* or *The Wizard of Oz*. If you ask my mom, she'll deny any awareness of our choice of film. She'll probably also deny that on our *daily* stop at McDonalds, she'd buy me four hashbrowns. Nothing like fear and greasy carbs to stimulate a young mind headed off to learn geometry and practice the saxophone.

Man, I was weird. But not outwardly weird. I hid it well. To the outside world I was an innocent and pure lil peanut. Yes, all according to plan.

In the midst of watching as many scary movies as I could, and staying in the lane of spookiness, I happened upon astral traveling, also known as astral projection. It snuck up on me, but I was happily surprised by it. It first happened by accident, and when I realized what exactly it was, I worked to control the ability. I'll give you the low down on astral traveling if you're unaware. As with all esoteric matters, astral traveling has different understandings and meanings throughout the many religions and cultures and their histories that saturate our physical reality. In my current understanding, we are existing on the physical plane running around in our very physical bodies with 3-dimensional perceptions. The physical plane is the lowest density of all the planes. Meaning, we are heavy, heavy bodies ruled by heavy emotions. The astral plane is the second densest plane; the next plane up. Astral traveling is when a light part of your being rises from your dense, physical body, leaving the physical plane and floating on to the astral plane. The astral plane is a replica of our physical plane, but with so much more. More activity happening, and more beings to cause that activity.

Astral traveling can occur while you are conscious enough to understand what is happening, but it can also happen uncontrollably, by accident. I have been on both sides of that spectrum, and let me tell you, conscious, controllable astral traveling is the bees' knees.

When I first began attempting to astral travel, I would lay atop my bed with only my feet covered, to ward off the demons that wanted to tickle them. With some sort of hypnotic, lulling music playing through my headphones, I would enter into a meditative state. The idea was to allow my physical body to fall asleep while my consciousness remained aware. A difficult feat. Most times when I would purposefully try to astral travel, I'd enter into a meditative state that had my entire body buzzing. I'd experience quick spasms of a feeling that I relate to floating. But every time I'd feel lighter than my physical body, like some kind of experience was imminent, my heart rate would speed up and I'd come out of the stupor. It was a fickle process of trying to balance deep relaxation and the excitement of the unknown. Like anything, it took practice and discipline.

Intentional astral traveling took a long time to harness. But my soul knew how to make it happen, whether my conscious mind was aware of that or not. It seemed that the answer was in staying detached from the outcome, having no expectations. I can't count the number of times that I would fall asleep, and suddenly gain awareness into the feeling of my astral body lifting up and out of my physical body. Always when I was least expecting it. My hands would pop out first. If I focused, I could sense my physical hands still resting on the bed while a lighter part of my being was rising. My hands were always the first to go, but the rest of my astral body followed suit. Instead of simply rising from my physical body, I usually found my astral body taking on the effective and, apparently, natural technique of rolling itself out. Flinging itself from my physical body, off my bed, and onto the floor. It was more graceful than it sounds. My astral body was light and soft and just not physical in the slightest. No bumps, no bruises.

When I had completely dislocated from my physical body, I was free to fly as far and wide as I pleased. Though for some reason in my past explorations I have never strayed too far from what I knew. You could typically find me ambling around one of my homes or the cities nearby. The deal with the astral plane is that there are other beings and entities that are much more "real". Meaning if you're exploring the astral plane, you're going to be exposed to everything more so than on our physical plane. If you have a vibration of fear, you will be surrounded by similar low vibrating energies and beings. In my past explorations, I have experienced a certain level of discomfort each time I traveled while fully aware. So to wander further meant to come across things I may not have been ready for. Things that matched my fear-based frequency. Things that I wanted no interaction with. I think subconsciously I must have known my limits. High-five for being *not* naive, Morgan!

Like my attempt to make hypnosis a fun and easy activity at slumber parties, I also introduced astral traveling. The notion was always exciting to the group, but the process of making it happen usually just led to us falling asleep early with no results, to our dismay, and my parents' infinite gratitude.

One night, a middle school sleepover was ensuing. Four of us girls were packed into my bedroom, scattered across piles of comforters, pillows, and air mattresses. The mood was serious. The only noise, a ticking of the clock echoing from the living room nearby. Each of us was zoned out, thinking we were on the precipice of reaching the astral plane. Except Jayden, who was not zoned out. She was instead very zoned in on how quiet and dark the room was. Out of the peaceful quiet came a soft cry for reassurance.

"Guys?" Jayden questioned.

None of us answered.

"GUYS?" Jayden questioned again, panic obviously taking itself up a notch.

I flipped on a lamp.

She started rambling in response, "I got really scared and then none of you answered so I thought you were all on the astral plane without me..."

Yet again, we remained quiet.

"Morgan?" Jayden whispered.

And as I take every opportunity I'm presented with, I did that slow robotic head turn, complete with wide, unblinking eyes, and whispered, "I'm not Morgan anymore".

What followed was Jayden freaking the hell out, my momma probably coming in, in her bathrobe and disheveled hair telling us to quiet down, and the sudden conclusion of astral traveling/slumber party mashups. The end.

Another facet of opening up to and embracing the unknown, the mystical, the supernatural, was the onset of clairvoyance. I've been working to strengthen my clairvoyant abilities since I was tiny and innocent; ever since my momma shared her abilities. I wanted to be just like her. So, when I discovered that I had the capability to harness the same clairvoyant abilities, or seeing the future and knowing beyond normal capacity, I worked to cultivate it. My momma and I used to make a game out of having these psychic abilities when neither of us could fall asleep. We'd take turns projecting numbers up onto the ceiling or sending them directly to each other's mind. We'd pick a number 1-10 and envision it big and bright, spread out across the ceiling. Or we'd repeat the number in our head while sending the thought of it to one another. We'd guess the first number that came to mind, finding that we were right more often than not. We were likened to professionals, able to guess the numbers on our first try multiple times in a row. But it turns out that my momma had a slight advantage. Also known as cheating. To my momma, it was simply using her resources.

"They're showing me a verse in the Bible with a number six. Is it six?"

I huffed, "who is 'they'? Are spirits helping you?" I shook my fist towards the sky.

Suffice to say, I didn't get to make the rules. My momma, with the help of her teammates, continued guessing my numbers.

Those first few years of opening up to the supernatural, metaphysical, whatever name you want to apply to it, were cultivated by my momma. The stories and experiences and present knowledge that she shared so openly and honestly, through her personal journey with the unknown, laid the foundation for my constant desire for constant exploration and constant expansion. That means I was *constantly* asking my momma questions. Bless her for putting up with that. Patience is a virtue that I do not easily muster. On the contrary, it's one of the many, many things that I'm working on everyday.

On the topic of my momma sharing her experiences so openly, I automatically think of a fitting story. The first story I vividly remember her sharing on the topic of spirits. Or, more specifically, on spirits that were in our house. How backwards is that? My momma trying to convince me, the nine-year-old, that the house was haunted. Although not much convincing was needed. I hold this experience close to me, as it became the first validation that I received on the realness of spirits *without* the help of my momma and her abilities. And I have a picture to prove it!

It was 2009, and a slumber party was happening at my house. My two besties, Jayden and Eva, were staying over. Most of the night was occupied by my momma recounting stories of spirits and prophetic experiences. This was right around the time that she made her abilities known and, just like me, my friends were always mystified and curious. Teetering on the edge of scared disbelief and excited wonder.

My momma began relaying the history of the old victorian home we were living in. Though she owned it as a three-apartment rental property, passed down to her from my great-grandfather, Poppy, it once belonged to the wealthiest man in Marinette, WI. His name was Isaac Stephenson. You can find that moniker plastered on many of the prominent establishments throughout town. The Stephenson National Bank, Stephenson Island, and my personal favorite, the Stephenson Public Library. He was a Senator, and a very successful businessman. And that's about the extent of my research, courtesy of Wikipedia. The home was built for him, and wasn't always divided into three units but instead was grand and beautiful and whole. A victorian home that creepy old-timey children could only dream of. Of course, this was back in the 1800's. Which brings us to how exactly this became a ghost story worth sharing.

"He's here right now. I'm not sure why..." my momma wondered out loud, "I really don't know why, but he's hanging around. I can see him right now, standing in the doorway."

Us girls squinted hard.

Enter from stage right, my brother. My brother, who is nothing if not a straightforward instigator, sashayed from the shadows hungry for some blood.

"Hello Isaac Stephenson, get the hell out of my house," he demanded. Tanner continued with a whole monologue of goofy entitlement, in his particular vernacular that is much more colorful than mine.

You gonna take that, Isaac? The energy in the room changed after choice words were flung at Isaac Stephenson. Even I could pick up on the thick energy that was building. We suddenly felt uncomfortable, like shiznit was getting real. I raised my eyebrows, expecting a physical, yet invisible, rebuttal to ensue.

My momma laughed nervously at Tanner's antics, "Tanner, buddy, knock it off. He does not like that one bit."

As my brother worked to rile big, bad Isaac up...it, well, worked. Isaac Stephenson's energy would intensify, allowing him to become bolder and brighter. My momma apologized on Tanner's behalf as Tanner downed a Dr. Pepper, crushed it against his head, and retreated back to the dark corners of the house to play video games. We continued on with our night, the excitement far from over.

Soon my momma tired from talking, but as a result of being eleven-year-olds, we tired from nothing. We were the dominant species. Unmatched by any other. So with our restlessness, Jayden, Eva, and I decided we needed to do something to further explore the mystery of the old Victorian house and the wealthy man who may or may not still walk the halls. It was like we three were collectively Nancy Drew. Keeping with the theme of the night, spookiness, we ventured into the basement to pull up the floorboards and dig beneath them. I had remembered a conversation I overheard between my momma and my Aunty Tami, another psychic medium in the family. They intuitively felt that physical items were buried in the basement, covered up by uneven floorboards. Small knick-knacks, letters, *diaries*!

"If you wreck those boards or make a huge mess, you're going to be in trouble," my momma stated in her most serious tone. But that was all the confirmation we needed. We three raced down the rickety, narrow stairs, across dusty cement floors, and past boarded up rooms that held unknown items. We set a flash light up and put our digging tools to work once the loose floorboards were lifted. All the while, every part of the basement's spooky atmosphere was setting us off. The single light bulb that lit up only a small portion of the basement would flick, and we'd shriek. A save-yourself mentality in full effect, we'd dash to the stairs only to sneak back down when the coast seemed clear. Then a strange noise would manifest and we'd run the whole thing again. But eventually we put our big girl pants on and made some real progress in the glow of the SYFY yellow. I'm sure my momma was grateful for the quiet time upstairs, considering we spent hours down in the basement that night. And after those few hours, we hadn't found anything except animal bones, and there was nothing romantic about animal bones.

The following weekend I had Jayden and Eva over again. And, no surprise, we found ourselves in the basement again. This time we wanted *more*. And this time we wanted *more* with less *work*. We decided to take my mom's fancy camera and try to capture those who lurked in the shadows…no, not Tanner. No corner of the basement was left untouched by our amateur photography skills. When we concluded our investigation, we huddled around the camera display screen to examine our findings. Nothing, nothing, nothing, next, sigh, and *then*.

"Wait, what is that?" Eva pointed out. We collectively stilled and looked deeper into the picture. There. I grappled for the camera and bolted up the stairs two at a time, my destination: our desktop computer.

"What? WHAT?" Jayden and Eva yelled from close behind, chasing me up the decrepit stairs two at a time. As fast my little nubby fingers could muster, I typed the name Isaac Stephenson into the search bar. I clicked the first image that popped up and stared in wide-eyed disbelief. In one of the many pictures we had taken, we captured an anomaly. But it wasn't an anomaly at all, and we had the internet to thank for that conclusion. It was the big man himself, Isaac Stephenson, appearing to us on my mom's camera. I was freaking the fudge out, as eleven-year-old Morgan would say. I spent the next couple years sharing the picture with every new acquaintance.

After reflecting, the "crazy phenomena" that has ensued in my life was all prefaced in my earlier years by the fascinations and curiosities that intrinsically existed within me. The Universe was foreshadowing what was to come through my hobbies, affinity for the unknown, and everyday experiences. Man, I want to be as great an author as the Universe some day.

Slowly but surely I was recognizing the world around me and the curious experiences for what it all truly meant: the beginning of the end. Bum bum BUM! I mean that in the best way possible. My spiritual journey had commenced, sending "normalcy" packing and sending me running for the hills a time or two in the years to come. And though I believe that time is not linear as we perceive it in this current "reality", I *do* realize that if I want to keep this tell-all in a comprehensible order, then I'm getting a little ahead of myself. That means, as much as I'd like to keep it buried away, the next chapter takes place throughout my years in middle school.

      I think I just heard the collective consciousness cringe. Or maybe it was just me... Anyways.

♡ Chapter 3 ♡

Thank the God Source for Puberty!

Middle school conjures up a lot of nostalgic memories. Like "missing the bus" when it rolled around, try as I might to get a move on. Or gym class, which was my favorite part of the day. Nothing like letting out a can of whoop ass in the form of a dodgeball. Yes, it was a simpler time. A time when you could eat as much as you wanted only to burn the calories off by the end of recess. But my time as a young kiddo in middle school wasn't only characterized by cutesy things like slumber parties where we took on the role of each spice girl. I was sporty-spice. My prepubescent, highly important developmental years, as touched on in the previous chapter, were the kickoff of a lifelong, intentional spiritual journey.

My exposure to spirituality at this point in time had less to do with my own personal, slowly developing abilities, and more to do with quick glimpses provided by my momma and my passed-over loved ones. My momma never held back a message that came through for me, regardless of the endless berating I did for more. And my passed loved ones never skimped on the messages. In retrospect, I was incredibly lucky to hear validating and supportive messages from loved ones who I thought I had heard the last from. Incredibly lucky, I was, to have a momma and confidant who encouraged my curiosity and spiritual expansion. Especially during a critical time of development, when insecurities start to appear and the voice inside your head kicks the meanness up a notch. And thank you to my crossed-over loved ones, who introduced me to the wonder of signs, amongst many other forms of magic.

I believe signs, or messages from the Universe and the beautiful beings that comprise it, are always taking shape and appearing before us. Ask the people around me, and they'll tell you that I take everything as a sign. Even the things that are absolutely not signs. Of course they're signs, too. It's our responsibility to acknowledge these signs, when we're ready to resonate with them. We may not be ready at the same time, but that's neither here nor there. Spiritual journeys are subjective, and all the while spiritual expansion is constant.

In the beginning, signs were most plentiful above all else; a means to corral me onto my soul's path of exploring the curiosity of the spiritual. These tidbits of information, important messages, and little hellos came from loved ones; family and friends that have passed on, spirit guides, higher beings of all sorts, and the power of the Universe as a collective. Yes, the Universe loves you. It just also loves balance and sometimes that won't seemingly play in your favor. But it's all love, baby.

I remember being indoctrinated into the experience of receiving signs, one summer weekend in the early years of middle school. My family was packed into our car with a cooler stocked full of munchies, headed a few hours out of town. We spent a lot of weekends in the same manner. Tanner was on a traveling baseball team, and therefore we traveled.

We were headed to Dodgeville, which was about four hours from where we lived. Windows rolled down, Dad taking peaks at the printed out MapQuest directions, because as I have said already, it was a much simpler time. We made it to our hotel where we congregated with the other baseball players and their families; where I scoped out the cutie-patooties and the vending machine. When the excited chatter about the weekend tournament came to a close, we found our beds and hit the hay. I had a good friend in tow that weekend, so we were designated to the floor with a pile of pillows and blankets. It felt like I was camping, which my family never did although I pushed the idea more than once. Even at a young age I loved being on the move, and didn't require more than a space to sprawl at the end of the day. So I closed my eyes and allowed sleep to take me. The faster I fell asleep, the faster I could get up and order cheesy nachos from the ballpark concession stand.

Flash forward to 6am that next morning. Everyone was still sleeping except me. While they slumbered peacefully, I stumbled around the room haphazardly, trying to stir someone from their sleep without having to actually wake someone up. Please someone wake up, I pleaded to my sleeping family. I was suffering from the aftershock of the most intense dream I had been exposed to in all of my eleven years. It went like this:

I was aware I was sleeping. That's actually the first time I can remember having full awareness in a dream. The setting was beautiful, not something that would typically cause fear. The buildings that surrounded me were Roman architecture inspired; cream in color with large columns and even larger steps that led to ornately-detailed doorways. The ground beneath me was marble tile and the sky above me, the brightest blue, devoid of any clouds. People walked around casually, scattered here and there throughout the square I stood in. It was peaceful and pure, unlike any setting I had seen before. And because the dream was so vivid, my senses were heightened. So when someone yelled out, "look up at the sky!", I felt fearful at the loud cry from a random passerby that brought all others around me to a halt. I snapped my attention to the sky, where a mass hoard of *balloons* of all colors were floating in unison. The other bystanders looked on, as I did, curious of what was happening. And then someone yelled, "watch out!" The balloons, still packed tightly together, zoomed across the sky with precision not known to most balloons. As though they were controlled by a remote, their direction changed by 90 degrees. They were rushing towards me from high in the sky, plummeting down to the ground when I woke up back on the floor of the hotel room. I shot up from under the covers, hopping over my friend, and threw the curtains open to check the morning sky. No balloons. Why was I heavy-breathing? Ridiculous, Morgan. You are not scared of balloons. But I peeked out the window one more time to make sure there was nothing out of the norm. The dream really shook me, but how could I make my family understand the fear that it caused? The colors were so bright. I was so hyperaware. The balloons looked like they were trying to attack me. Who were all those people? And where was I?

  So there I was at 6am, pacing and causing random noises to hopefully wake my family up in the most passive way. Lucky me, the alarm went off shortly after I awoke. Everyone began moving and shaking, preparing for the long day. And there I was, rocking in the corner furthest from the window. Eventually I cozied up to my momma who was fixing her hair in the mirror.

  "Momma," I whispered, "I had a bad dream."

  I went on to explain what had transpired in my dream state. She understood that the vividity had caused an unusual response in me, and simply validated and honored my experience. I felt safe for the time being, reassured that balloons would not target me once I walked out the hotel doors.

  At the baseball fields that day, my friend and I found ourselves bored after the second game. We retreated to an open park area behind the outfield fence of the ballpark my brother was playing on. We brought over a blanket and some munchies and started doing middle school girl things, like charwheels and what not. My friend collapsed on the blanket in exhaustion. I collapsed onto my stomach in the opposite direction. And from the opposite direction that I faced, far off in the distance, a mirage brought on by the summer heat began to manifest. I leaned onto my elbows and squinted in disbelief. Say it isn't so! What I thought was a mirage was instead a single red balloon. I rubbed my eyes dramatically like they do in cartoons, and looked again. Yes, still a balloon, and this time it was closer. It floated along the outside of the outfield fence, from around the corner of the field. At that point in the day, my friend had already heard about my dream so I smacked her leg repeatedly until she looked my way.

    We stared at each other wide eyed, and then slowly looked back towards the single red balloon floating our way. Imagine my reaction when from around the corner, a half-dozen more balloons tauntingly made their way along the fence, static cling keeping them from attacking. I remember running away from our spot on the blanket while my friend laughed at the absurdity of the situation. But even she was impressed by the parallel between my dream and now real life. When I realized the balloons were not fast moving or precise in the slightest, my friend and I took a stroll around the corner of the outfield fence to investigate the origin of the mysterious balloons. We were dumbfounded to find no plausible explanation. Houses were not near enough to warrant a collective of balloons to float all the way to the fence. As for people, my friend and I were the only ones in the vicinity.

    We ran back to the bleachers in search of my momma and dad to share about the balloons and, further, the fact that the simulation was dismantling itself as we spoke.

    "You know, Morgan," my momma whispered between cheers from the crowd, "today is actually one year since your Grandpa Russell passed away. Maybe these are a sign from him."

    You're telling me that my Grandpa Russell, who had passed a year prior, was the evil mastermind behind the chilling and prominent experience? Genius. It was as though he was really trying to make the idea of balloons stick in my mind. And it worked, because to this day I can't see a balloon without automatically recalling the personage of my Grandpa Russell in my head and my heart. After that weekend in Dodgeville, I increasingly began to recognize signs from my Grandpa Russell in the form of balloons, amongst other objects and experiences.

The first time I recognized a sign that was being gifted to me was still within those foggy years of middle school. I've tried to hide that time period away in the dark depths of my mind, but every once in a while an awkward prepubescent memory will surface. During this particular time, I was freaking out about an upcoming middle school band concert that I'd be playing in. Somewhere along the way in my childhood, standing before an expecting crowd became terrifying to me. This from the girl who performed in musicals and talent shows with vigor and pizzazz earlier on. You couldn't even mention the word "presentation" without a tidal wave of dread wracking my body. I still have nightmares centered around hearing the teacher explain our next presentation project, and I am a grown woman. So, staying in the lane of dramatics, I really didn't know if I was going to survive that 7th grade band concert. But never fear, for even pre-spiritual Morgan had the Universe on her side, AKA: my Grandpa Russell. I was shaking like a dog when I walked with my class onto the theater stage, alto saxophone in hand. I know, I'm ridiculous. I took my seat and whispered a quick request to my Grandpa Russell to make the power go out or something to save me from that hell. And while I was accepting my defeat, lining up my sheet music on the stand before me, and coming to terms with my imminent doom, something told me to look up. Floating directly above me in the stage rafters was a single balloon on a string. A mother-lovin' balloon. I cackled at the absurdity and the quick reassurance that I was given. It was as if my Grandpa Russell was saying, "you are not alone, Patootie! Now play the hell outta that saxophone."

Apparently that was all I needed to instill the adequate amount of cool, calm, and collected within me. I positioned my fingers, which were no longer trembling, on the appropriate keys and played for my Grandpa Russell. Man, there was still so much that I didn't know about the Universe and how it worked. But I did know that I would never be alone on the spiritual journey that was just beginning for me.

My Grandpa Russell has been cheering me on from somewhere far better for years now in the form of balloons, pennies, visitations, and other creative ways that are still being discovered. Back then I was asking for signs of reassurance that I'd survive yet another dreaded band concert. Today it's more so asking for signs of validation that I'm on the right track and doing the Universe and my highest self justice. My Grandpa Russell is probably just about done with me and my constant questioning at this point. Somebody get that guy a pair of ear plugs! Lord knows I'm a curious one.

* * * * *

That time of my life was mild in comparison to what was to come. But I still experienced some effects of the imminent expansion of my spiritual abilities. Like realizing I could pick up on people's emotions effortlessly. It was as simple as walking into a room and knowing that my parents had been arguing, or that someone was hiding a secret from me. My empathic abilities were blooming.

I also did a lot of sleep walking at this time in my life. I'd wake up to find myself downstairs on the couch in our living room with the computer room light turned on and my closet door open and my pillows strewn around my room and so forth. But my brother was an even more notorious sleepwalker than I was. One night he ran through the house in his sleep, running outside where my momma found him standing, asleep, on the other side of the front door.

To add onto the weird sleeping activities, I accidentally astral traveled just about every other night. It wasn't my favorite thing in the world to find awareness with half of my body paralyzed, while my astral legs had the ability to flounder. I remember one night feeling totally and utterly out of control. I was just trying to get some z's for my tired physical body that was burnt out from a rec league soccer game, but alas my spirit was restless. I'd doze blissfully into the sleepies, only to find myself a moment later payalyzed, stuck between the physical plane and the astral realm. I'd scan the room weakly, unable to turn my head from where it rested on the pillow. Immediately my eyes zoned in on a dark figure standing at the end of my bed. A mass of blackness, much darker than the shadows that filled my room in the night. The figure lacked any defined characteristics, other than being human-like in shape. But it wasn't a human, and I wasn't sticking around to inquire further. I snapped my eyes shut and mentally worked to shake the feeling back into my physical body. Hurry up before the dark nondescript figure gets me! Slowly I regained the ability to move my hands, and then my arms, and eventually my entire body. When the last inch of control was regained, I bolted to the lightswitch. Every corner and space of my room was illuminated then, but no dark, nondescript figure remained. After checking under my bed, in my closet, and even the hallway outside my room, I made my way back under the covers and allowed my heart to stop pounding in my chest enough to slip back to sleep... only to come back into awareness a moment later, paralyzed once again. For a second, I refused to look, knowing exactly what was on the other side of my closed eyelids. But because you just feel compelled to look in those kinds of moments, that's what I had to do. The dark figure was now at the side of my bed, only an arm's length away. The perfect distance to steal my soul. Not today, Satan. I mentally worked to shake myself with all of the might stored inside my tiny body, eyes glued shut in complete fight mode. Or is that flight? Regardless, I was doing the most in my paralyzed state to combat the situation. A prayer that I had developed around that same point in my life went off automatically in my head.

"God, Jesus, mother of God Azna, Archangel Michael, my loved ones from this life and my past lives, spirit guides, guardian angels, please protect me with the white light. Make me a beacon of peace, light, and love."

I was shaking and praying, doing a lil exorcism on myself. Heavy-breathing, gaining control of my body once more and fully joining this physical plane again. Not even keeping my bedroom light on, along with my TV, could combat the pull to leave my body or fight off the fear-inducing figures that ensued. But it surely couldn't happen a third time. So I yanked the blanket up to cover all but my eyes, and once more allowed myself to cautiously drift back to sleep. And because it be like that sometimes, I came into awareness for the third time, paralyzed and pissed off. This time there was no dark, nondescript figure loitering about my bedroom. All seemed peaceful, except for my inability to move again which I could fix with ten seconds of mental fortitude and the intention of returning back to my physical body. But as I was about to start the eloquent process of mentally shaking myself to wake up, I was interrupted by a movement beneath my blankets on the edge of the bed. Still completely paralyzed, all I could do was watch as a snake-like movement made its way to the edge of the covers, and a mangled hand appeared from beneath. The hand, slowly crawling towards my face, quickly sent me inward. I was screaming that same prayer internally with more panic this time, and mentally shaking like my life depended on it. When I felt the slightest bit of control back in my body, I rolled from my bed onto the floor and crawled to the other end of the room. I spent the rest of the night camped out on the carpet, falling asleep only when I could no longer fight it. I've been a night owl ever since. But what I lacked in sleep, I made up for in really great organizational skills. Need me to come by and organize your closet between the hours of 11pm and 3am? Gimme a call, I have a lot of experience.

In the beginning, the things I saw were mostly in the middle of the night or due to astral travels. Unlike my momma, who saw things during the day and could harness the ability with at least a bit of grace. I was seeing things that just couldn't be validated by others, though my momma always honored my experiences. But my spiritual expansion continued on as it does, and soon enough I had my first experience with simultaneously seeing beyond and receiving validation from outside sources.

My momma and I were meeting my Aunty Tami for lunch at a quaint cafe near the marina in the next town over. The spot has outdoor seating on the front porch with a great view of the boats docked at the shore, and the sparkling water beyond. But on this day, we sat inside in a back corner near a staircase that was slightly shadowed; a staircase that was occupying my attention.

My Aunty Tami is my great aunt, a sister to my momma's momma, my Grandma Halfmann. The very same Grandma Halfmann who eventually plays a big role as a spiritual teacher from the other side. But I'm getting ahead of myself.

I have always loved visiting with my Aunty Tami and all of the energy and spunk she brings with her. She's a powerful woman who takes no shit, but incredibly kind and compassionate like any great empath. Her and my Uncle Jim owned a supper club as I was growing up. It was always a treat to visit their part of the family and finish with a yummy meal, paired with my drink of choice: a kitty cocktail and two maraschino cherries. I was a precocious child. But that day at the cafe my drink of choice was a hot chai tea latte in a big ole coffee cup. We three were planted around a table catching up. I mentioned briefly earlier that my Aunty Tami is also a psychic medium, as well as a reiki healer. The topic of conversation happening revolved around spirituality, but my attention was on the staircase. More specifically, what I saw on the staircase. Multiple times from the corner of my eye I had glimpsed what I thought was a young girl standing on the third step up. When I would turn to look, I'd only catch a fleeting image of the girl before the vision vanished.

"What do you see, Morgan?" my Aunty Tami questioned, pressing me for an answer that she already knew.

Timid me retreated inward slightly, not wanting to be wrong.

"A young girl…" I answered, though it was phrased more like a question rather than a statement.

"Yep! There's a young girl here. How old does she look?" she pressed.

"About 7 or 8 years old maybe!" I offered with greater confidence this time.

My Aunty Tami nodded knowingly. My momma smiled proudly. And I paused, reflectively, realizing that my abilities must be expanding and that's what they'd continue to do as time passed. That was my first experience seeing spirits and receiving validation. Surely, that would not be the last time. My momma and Aunty Tami continued on in conversation about the spirits they had encountered recently, and I sat bracing the chair I sat in, eyes growing wider and wider, reflecting on all of the scary movies I had watched and the gossip I had heard in my short lifetime on the topic of psychics and mediums. I felt a growing sense of overwhelm and discomfort and fear, but only until they brought out the New York cheesecake I ordered.

Nevertheless, I marched onward into the great unknown, too absorbed by my curiosity to contemplate the fear any further.

♡ Chapter 4 ♡

Like High School Musical But No Singing and Really Just Completely Different Entirely

Throughout my four years in high school, I was accessing untapped knowledge and abilities like it was my part-time job. And when I say that, I mean I was stumbling continuously into new unknowns. And by that of course I mean clumsily tripping, barely catching my footing, before face-planting into the next curious topic of discovery. It was never elegant, and not often planned. I think puberty is what kicked this spurt of spiritual awakening off. I can reflect back and acknowledge that there was definitely a positive correlation between my growing interest in boys and my spiritual abilities heightening.

Naturally it seemed that life had to throw a little bit more my way when I was already busy juggling homework, school sports, traveling team sports, extracurriculars, a social life, and sleep. Back then it felt like the Universe was testing my limits, but now I know that it was my trust in the Universe that was being tested. Even if I was unconscious to that understanding at the time. Divine timing is perfect. And divine timing said it was time for me to start sensing spirits in greater clarity, among experiencing many other super powers often associated with a spiritual awakening.

Ahh yes. Spirits. The catalysts for once upon a time being too scared to sleep at night, but ultimately, for the creation of this book; for the inspiration to pursue my passion of writing. I wouldn't constantly be questioning if I'm crazy if it weren't for these guys! In moments of fear or annoyance or excitement, I recorded my experiences. As a form of therapy, to remember for a rainy day, to keep track of my progress. My interactions with spirits became way too frequent at this point that I was left with no choice but to document everything. It helped me to stay collected. To feel in control.

There's a particular scene in every scary movie. The protagonist stares into a reflective surface, looks away for only a split second, and looks back to see the ghost behind them. That's what I expected on a daily basis, although the spirits weren't as visible and definitely not as malevolent. When I opened up at this time and was able to sense spirits more strongly than before, I quickly came to hate reflective surfaces. I could *feel* spirits nearby, next to me, behind me, and I thought I'd die on the spot and join them on a different plane or in a different dimension if I saw them in the reflection of the mirror. My skincare routine was atrocious for a few years. I did the most to avoid washing my face in the bathroom sink at night.

In my experience, spirits didn't usually make themselves known by appearing in mirrors, as Bloody Mary would have you believe as a kid. But as I became more comfortable with the uncomfortable, I *welcomed* the spooky, scary-movie-like experiences.

"Alright, now's your chance. If you want to scare me real good, capitalize on this moment in three, two, one," I whisper right before plunging my face into the sink. And because that's the energy that I was emitting, scary movie experiences happened upon me for the next few years. But we'll get to that eventually.

Ever since my momma allowed her abilities to take control, and encouraged my brother and I to open up as a result, our household has been welcoming in spirits on a daily basis. My momma was once the only host, but I was starting to learn the trade firsthand. While the years marched on in a linear fashion, as they do in this current reality, I marched along on my spiritual journey. And spirits marched alongside me from time to time, providing me experiences that would only lead to greater expansion.

Sometime during those four years in highschool, my momma met her husband, Todd, and from then on I lived in Coleman with my momma and Marinette with my dad. The two towns were only twenty minutes apart, and I loved the drive once I had my own car. Most of the experiences I write about during this period in my life took place wherever my mom was. I think us being in the same place created quite the beacon of light for spirits and other beings passing in the night. At my momma's house in Coleman, my days were normal from the moment my alarm went off in the morning, all the way until the sweet voice of Steve Harvey making some dirty joke on Family Feud lulled me to sleep. But my normal days would consist of a few disembodied voices and fleeting apparitions sprinkled in. To clarify, my developing mediumship didn't allow me to see spirits as physically as I would see living people around me. Only once in a blue moon has that happened. Spirits would be brief colors passing my field of vision. Hazy and transparent movement. Energy shifts in the form of light or heavier pressure. Cool breezes. Sudden emotional bouts that weren't mine. A random name or idea or image popping into the forefront of my mind, and so forth. The variation was endless. The creativity was remarkable.

Everyday we encountered spirits, whether they were people that we had known on this physical plane or those who we never had the pleasure of crossing paths with. They walked into our house, popped into our heads without notice, and even journeyed with us through our dreams.

Most of the time, it was only those momentary sensations that would alert me to the presence of a spirit. But these feelings were always accompanied by the secondary sensation that I wasn't alone. Comforting at times, and other times a bit off putting. I'm talking about you, creepy dude who stood in my bedroom doorway at night for weeks! As my abilities continued to expand, the indicators for a nearby spirit became more and more obvious. Goosebumps racking my body. The feeling of someone touching me; holding my hand, gently grabbing my forearm, or placing a hang on my back. When I felt these peculiar sensations, I'd smile and acknowledge the gentle connection; the respectful notice that they were near.

I found that spirits, like living people, had their own personalities and ways of presenting themselves. Let me rephrase that. I found that spirits retained the personalities that they likely carried in their lifetime on Earth. They're still the same people, just existing in a less dense form. Some were more passive, whereas others made themselves known in clear and obvious demonstrations. I can't tell you how many times I've heard knocks on my door, only to realize no one was there. No living, physical human that is. I can't count on my hands and toes the amount of times that I've heard someone call my name so clearly, or felt as though someone was shouting indecipherably to get my attention. And the last of "I can't explain how often this certain thing happened" goes on and on and on.

One time when I had a boyfriend over, one of my many suitors, my momma and him were deep in conversation about specific spirits that shared the house with us at the time when a cabinet door opened in front of us. We were taken off guard but not entirely surprised, because spirits like to make themselves known just as much as we love the validation that we're not crazy.

Those types of experiences seemed to follow us wherever we went. After my momma got remarried, we moved into our house in Coleman. A cute country house in a tiny village. Coleman is populated by 400 people, and 401 tractors that like to hold up traffic on the main road in town. If I never see a tractor again in this lifetime, it'll be too soon. Our house was tucked back behind some pine trees, and as you could imagine, a couple crops. The few acres that we lived on were wide open, surrounded on all sides by woods. The perfect setting for a horror film. Take the long driveway through the dense woods until you get to the very massive clearing in the middle of nowhere, with a lone, spooky farmhouse and an incredible lack of witnesses.

It was just as spooky on the inside as it was on the outside. Not in a threatening way, but in a charming, choose-your-own-adventure kind of way. The basement was finished, which was a dream, and had two bedrooms to choose from. I must have manifested this! Both bedrooms had a similar layout, so it really was just an eenie-meenie-minie-mo situation. Except for the fact that one of the bedrooms had a portal through which spirits and beings and energy freely passed in and out. It was unquestionable. Simply another feature that the house offered. Four bedrooms, one full bath, furnished basement, chill portal in the corner of the back bedroom in the basement. We could feel the push and pull of energy. The room felt immensely more "haunted" than any other area in the house. Beyond that, it made the room visibly foggy. The portal was hard to ignore, and especially hard to deny if you stepped into the room.

"That's it. That's the one," I stated to my momma, my mind set on the adventures I would have in the curious room with the perplexing portal. Me, still holding the energy of a scary movie protagonist. My momma shook her head, rejecting my claim.

"Nope, I've decided it's not happening. We're going to let the spirits have that room to themselves. They aren't going to want you in their space all of the time."

Way to make me feel like the young, bothersome sister, Momma. But she was genuinely adamant that I not take up residence in that room out of respect for the spirits. Soon enough I had no arguments on the topic. The activity in the house was constant, and a portal in my bedroom would not a happy camper make. Besides, I didn't need the portal a foot away from my bed to act as a magnet for on the move spirits and wandering energy. So I happily took up residence in the bedroom across the hall. We didn't often go into that spare bedroom. It only held random things like snowmobile gear, board games, candles, and a tanning bed. I gave up using the tanning bed real fast because every time I laid in it, I heard voices and felt people standing too close. Let me tell you, it is a very uncomfortable feeling lying butt naked in a room full of people. Especially when my bare feet were exposed at the end of the bed, innocently offering the dead to tickle them. I mean, it would be hard to pass that up if I were a spirit sharing a house with an on-edge teenage girl. It didn't help that lying in a tanning bed easily turns into a meditation session. The warmth of the rays and the peaceful hum of the fan blowing makes for a most wonderful zoning-out atmosphere. Which in turn entails a collective conference between the deceased and the newbie medium in training. Meditation leads to a heightened energetic frequency. A heightened energetic frequency leads to a heightened awareness. Heightened awareness leads to chit-chat through the threshold of here and there. A=B=C. The transitive property. And who said the things we learned in math class wouldn't matter? I did. That was definitely me.

So entering the room didn't happen too often. When we did need to get in the room, we habitually gave a short courtesy knock. It's like we had roommates. We never got an answer when we knocked, so we took that as an invitation in. They didn't make themselves known when we were respectful of their privacy, but they were known to get a little feisty when we forgot our manners. My momma has barged into the bedroom on numerous occasions, because she's a momma and that's what momma's do. When she would burst through the door, throwing the idea of privacy to the wind, the fire alarms in our house would go berserk for a few seconds. It happened multiple times, which is why I speak so flippantly about it. It was common. It even happened to me once.

"Ope! Sorry!" I said, quickly closing the door and bopping out of there.

So we knocked on that door. And soon spirits started knocking on doors and windows all throughout the house. I never understood what it was about the action of knocking that spirits seemed to get a kick out of. In my opinion, it's overdone. Cliche, if you will. Okay, fine, yes it scared me.

My momma and step-dad decided to zoom off to Cozumel for a week, leaving the dogs and me to fend for ourselves in the haunted house in the clearing in the woods. And as the dog-sitter, I couldn't just peel out of there when things got spooky. So I easily convinced Jayden to stay with me one night, saving me from the uncomfortable fate of having to stay home alone. The one other time I stayed home alone overnight looked a little something like me staying up until 4am doing the same puzzle twice and watching *The Notebook* three times. I was too on edge to sleep. We went to bed early that night since Jayden had to wake up extra early work the next day, bless her heart. It was still dark out that next morning when Jayden took off, and I was only half awake, sleeping in my momma's bedroom. I was about to fall back asleep when someone knocked on the patio door in her room. I sat up immediately as the rap of the door concluded. Slightly disturbed, I waited quietly and motionless. But I was too tired to care that much. In the early morning sleepiness, I convinced myself that it was the result of transitioning from dreaming to wakeful reality. When nothing more happened, I fell back onto the pillow and pulled the downy covers to my chin. It was five minutes later when another rap at the door sounded. I laid there, perfectly awake and immobile, listening to the knocking which was longer this time. It had a rhythm to it, far beyond the capacity of a wild animal interested confused by its reflection. I guess that meant no more sleep for me. Time to start my day! I sent a text to my momma, telling her about the knocking after looking out the window for any physical, living people.

Her response was, "Well peanut, someone definitely wants your attention. Don't answer the door."

In case you thought differently, there was no way in the nine circles of hell that I was opening the back patio door for mysterious knocking before the sun even came up.

"Hello? Who's there?"

"Yeah, it's just me, your friendly backwoods spirit coming to borrow some eggs."

How 'bout ya check the Piggly Wiggly down the road at a reasonable hour, eh?

*   *   *   *   *

My abilities began to open up at an increasing rate. I felt spirits and energy around me all of the time. Past the point of no return, I was. Sure of the destination, I was not. In my experience of spiritual expansion, my mediumistic and psychic abilities went hand in hand. So as my connection with spirit became stronger, so did my psychic senses.

Somedays I would put a great deal of effort into accessing my psychic abilities. I practiced and practiced and practiced, playing more Deal or No Deal online than I'd care to admit. Other times, I've been gifted with thoughts that badgered me until I acted on them.

One night in the fall of my senior year, I was home with my momma watching a storm get closer. The air was buzzing with that eerie calmness. An energy that was almost physically tangible. The wind was violently shaking the trees. The sky, a masterpiece of purple, pink, black, and yellow. The dude on the weather channel informed us the storm would be severe, but it wasn't anything we were worried about. It didn't seem out of the norm for fall in Wisconsin. Recently we had gotten ducks and chickens though, and I had this bad feeling about leaving them out in their pens for the storm. They had experienced storms before, but I couldn't shake the nagging idea in my head that something bad was going to happen. They were still delicate things after all. Little, vulnerable babies that needed to be protected.

"Momma, do you think we should move the chickens and ducks into the shed?" I asked, pacing from window to window, watching trees bend and leaves fly haphazardly.

My momma thought about it for a moment, "No, they should be alright outside in their pens."

The pens were two identical, stereotypical red chicken coops. Each was big enough to provide shelter to all of the chickens and ducks. Still, I felt that was the wrong choice. As the storm got closer, the wind picking up even more, I mentioned it to my momma again.

"I really think we should move them into the shed."

"Alright," she relented, "let's go check on them before the rain hits us."

So we ambled outside into the mess of wind that was building in intensity. The rain hadn't started yet, but it was imminent if you asked the dark clouds overhead. And not a moment later, as we reached the chicken coops, it began to pour. It was like that giant bucket at water parks that fills up with water until it gets to a tipping point. Buckets were collectively falling on us. We were drenched in a matter of seconds. Thunder boomed, challenging us to retreat. My momma and I exchanged frantic looks, and then we exchanged frantic looks with the equally, if not more, frazzled chicks and ducklings.

"Let's get all of them into the coops!" My momma yelled over the wind and the rain, the thunder and the lightning.

You should have seen us two, soaked and frantic, chasing the ducklings and chicks around their muddy fenced-in areas, trying to catch and deliver them to safety. It would have been funny if the storm wasn't becoming increasingly wicked. The rain was coming down so heavy at this point it was like we were basically swimming.

"Try saving your precious chicks and ducklings now without *vision*," I could hear my concocted version of the Universe's alter-ego taunting us.

We had about half the chicks and ducklings in their coops when the tree branches above us started to bend and snap. Just like Reese Witherspoon in *Legally Blonde 1* and *2*. My momma and I paused briefly to exchange frantic looks again before we sprung into action.

"We need to get them into the shed!" I yelled above all the noise, freaked out for not only the chicks and ducklings, but also for my momma and I because the weather man had it right when he said the storm was severe. But you know people from the midwest. We love to set up our lawn chairs in the garage and watch the storm violently pass through.

We started furiously grabbing at the chicks and ducklings from inside the coops. And you'd think with the threatening onslaught of torrential rain, constantly clapping of thunder, and the bend and snap that was taking place six feet above the birds, that they would be grateful for the familiar hands reaching in to save them. That was not the case. The birds did the most to make it difficult. But we'd finally get a hold of one and run it into our shed victoriously, which was a giant, stury, red barn. I had a duckling in each hand, and pretty much flung both of them into the shed once I made it through the door. When I ran back outside, I found my momma barely holding one of the coops down on the ground. Thinking back on the memory makes me laugh at how ridiculous and dramatic it was. It was wholesome family movie material. Things were escalating, until my momma was literally holding the situation together with her hands, feet, and motherly nature. The coop was being torn into pieces by the wind, but she had her whole body sprawled out over it to the best of her ability to keep the birds safe. Scraps of trim were flying off the coop. The thin walls were splintering. At that point, I ran into the shed and grabbed the first box I could find. I ran it back out to my momma and made her switch places with me. While I held up the coop in the same fashion she did, she threw chicks and ducklings into the box until it was overloaded. They could handle being a little squished and soggy, because my momma and I sure as hell could not handle the idea of those babies being tossed around by the heavy wind.

"GET THEM INTO THE SHED!" I yelled to my momma, in dramatic fashion with the wind whipping through my hair and fierce love for those babies in my heart. We heard a loud crazy and both looked up. A heavy branch was directly above the coop, threatening to fall down. My mom grabbed at the birds more frantically. Sticks started flying through the air. Considerably sized branches. And the big branch above us wasn't putting up much of a fight against the wind either.

"GET IN THE SHED! I GOT THE REST!" I yelled over the storm.

There were only a few left scrambling for dear life around the coop, and my momma already had a box full ready to be taken to safety.

"BE CAREFUL!" my momma yelled, running off and stumbling to get the birds into the shed. Sticks were flying by in every direction. They whipped past my momma as she fought to get back into the shed, and they whipped past me as I grabbed the last of the chicks ducklings. I had two birds in my arms, two very uncomplacent birds. Just one more. Stop running you little stinker, I'm trying to help you! And when I was finally able to snatch the last chick, I backed away from the coop, releasing it to the fury of the wind. Up until that point I had been holding it down in some weird manner with my legs and feet like the most serious game of Twister. And when I stepped back, the wind wasted no time in sweeping the structure up off the ground and utterly dismantling it. The three birds and I were wide-eyed, heavy breathing together at this point.

I stumbled into the shed, and set the birds free in a makeshift pen my momma had quickly manufactured from boxes and buckets and other odd objects laying about. We looked at each other in disbelief, each on the brink of a chaotic laughing fit. We caught our breath eventually and waited out the rest of the storm in the shed, which lasted another twenty minutes. Once the rain stopped pattering violently on the tin roof, we stepped out into the yard.

Parts of our white-picket fence were scattered around the yard, robust trees had fallen in the woods behind our house, and heavy metal sheets that were laid out on a trailer had blown about fifty feet from where they were piled.

"Did a freaking tornado go through?" my momma asked as we continued to take in the disarray.

We could not believe how crazy things had gotten. It was a 1 to 10 real quick kind of situation.

"Imagine if we didn't go out and check on them when we did," my momma quipped, motioning to the birds, "you had a feeling that it wasn't going to end well. You knew. I'm happy we were able to save them."

I was happy too. Relieved. But I don't think the chicks or ducklings could have cared less about our heroic acts. They still run away from me today when I get too close.

So sometimes the quick thoughts that passed through my head allowed me to help others, and sometimes I was given a little help myself. When I was in high school sitting in class, for instance, I'd know quite often when a teacher was going to call on me. I could even tell sometimes how many people a teacher was going to call on before they'd call on me. It usually gave me time to prepare my answer. But even when I knew ahead of time that my math teacher was targeting me, I would still desperately flounder for an answer. The Socratic method is evil, Mr. Furton. Evil but, I will admit, highly effective. I worked on homework for that class after school at my kitchen table until I cried. I'm a right-brained thinker, not left.

* * * * *

Discipline has always been difficult for me. I mean, come on, I'm a Sagittarius. What would you expect? A Sagittarius is the embodiment of freedom, and I *do* enjoy being free, expansive, and disorderly! But beyond me making light of the situation and using my sun sign as a defense against my shortcomings, it was truly evident that I needed to incorporate more discipline into my quickly expanding spiritual lifestyle. Around this time I began to focus on discipline in the form of meditation. All of the articles I had read on the internet about spiritual awakening directed me back to meditation. *Curses!* For someone like me, who had diagnosed ADHD and couldn't easily focus, meditation was not only boring but just flat out difficult. I'm sure many, at one time or another, could raise a glass to that.

Amidst my spiritual journey, meditation was a journey in and of itself. A sidequest, if you will. It was a dance of what seemed to be progress and regression, though I was constantly expanding whether it felt that way or not. Some days I prioritized meditation more, some days less. I have discovered that this ebbing and flowing of discipline and development is a normal characteristic of spiritual journeying. And therefore, I march on doing the best I can. Prior to my personal experiences with meditation I read the grocery list of reasons that convince people to meditate. Reducing anxiety, lengthening your attention span, encouraging emotional wellbeing and greater self-awareness, raising your energetic frequency, and so on. These were attractive benefits, that's for sure. But I often looked at those who advocated for meditation as being slightly hoity toity. Turns out that was a projection I placed onto them due to my own feelings of inferiority that I didn't realize I had. And after getting over my own ego and embracing meditation, I joined the advocates and now encourage meditation for everyone.

Meditation wasn't easy for me in the beginning. I was a perfectionist who felt that there was a right way to meditate and, per duality, a wrong way. Thoughts that I believed had absolutely no right to pop up in my fickle human brain during meditation did just that, and it exasperated me. No, it enraged me. I would literally huff in anger when I couldn't experience a "proper meditation". Here's some of the best advice I have received in this lifetime. There is no "right" way to meditate. Whatever your meditation experience looks and feels like is absolutely perfect. The saying goes "I wish I knew then what I know now", but my expansion was in the rollercoaster of highs and lows; trial and error'ing my way to where I am now.

So at that time in my life, I was more rigid in following structured meditation techniques, as I hadn't ascertained what felt right for me personally yet. I encourage you to explore the multitude of commonly known meditation techniques to further your understanding of mindfulness and to find what does and doesn't resonate with you. That being said, what you resonate with will change as often as the weather in Wisconsin.

While in high school, when I could still my always-moving body enough to sit and be mindful, I typically followed a detail-oriented meditation scenario that I carefully concocted to hold my focus. In the beginning especially, personally crafted meditation processes are very helpful in establishing routine and flow. It's like having training wheels that get you up and moving. Phase one of delving into meditation was finding a way to silence the outside world. My meditation process helped me to keep my internal world separate from the external world for a short time, simply because I created a bunch of visual steps in my mind's eye. I know, purposely creating stimuli in your mind is not the point of meditation, but it was an important step for me and my hyperactivity.

As I said, the meditation process I used was delicately crafted. I would close my eyes, whether lying beneath the covers on my bed or sitting somewhere that I wouldn't be disturbed. I took some deep breaths, in through my nose and out through my mouth. My stomach extended as I breathed in, and deflated as I released my breath. When I felt calm enough, I invited in one of my angels who I knew by name from a fleeting dream that stuck with me. Bartholomew. He gathered all of the negative energy that I carried with me, and stuffed what I envisioned as dark clumpy matter into a large burlap sack. I would imagine shaking the dark clumpy matter off of my body, as well as unhinging the top of my head and allowing Bartholomew to dive in with his lovely, angelic hands to collect all of the negative energy. When he had collected every last clump of dark matter, Bartholomew floated away with a grace unknown to humans, burlap sack thrown over his shoulder, headed to the heavens for purification. I always gave him a lil wave on his way out. Then, because I am detail-oriented, I envisioned myself taking a small broom and sweeping out whatever was left in my head. A stray-thought here, some cobwebs in the corner. When my head was empty, I let white light create a channel from the heavens directly into my unhinged head, passing through my crown chakra, which is the energy center on the crown of your head. After this clean-up was taken care of, I envisioned myself on a passenger train, seated in one of those little rooms with cushioned booths and a big window to gaze out romantically at the passing countryside. Pretty much like the train in the *Harry Potter* series. Actually, exactly like the train in the *Harry Potter* series. I realized over time that it was the exact train I envisioned. I sat on one of the comfy seats and looked out the window for a while, pulled in by the scenery. The scenery I envisioned was stolen from the movie, as well. While I stared longingly out the window, l allowed random thoughts to come to my mind. If they were only passing thoughts that needed a quick moment of acknowledgement, I gave them the attention and then allowed them to slip out through a crack in the window. During that part of the meditation, I also invited anyone to come pop a squat if they felt so inclined. I asked my spirit guides, guardian angels, and loved ones to only allow in those who were there for the most benevolent reason. And then I patiently waited for someone to amble on in. Sometimes I wonder if my mind created those people that sat across from me, and other times I was so zoned out that I myself was surprised when someone appeared before me in my mind's eye on the Hogwarts Express. I didn't have visitors stop by too often during these train meditations. I was primarily left to myself and my passing thoughts, which was the perfect experience for me in my early spiritual development as my mind was constantly on overdrive. When alone, images and ideas would fly through my head at a mile per minute. Sure, it could be chocked up to hypnagogic hallucinations but also, it could be the power of meditation and the innate spiritual connection to source that we're all privy to. Those visions that would appear in my mind's eye came and went and, oftentimes, I'd forget the vision a second after it disappeared. What did I see? It felt important but my consciousness didn't have a grasp on it tight enough. To my subconscious, it went. But every once in a while I would latch onto a vivid visual or a word that I heard. Most of the time at the conclusion of my meditation I would find some sort of validation to the images or terms, whether a connection was validated through my momma or the internet. I'd hear terms that I hadn't known previously or see images that I could pull up online by describing their details. Those early meditations alternated between me being completely and fully aware, and just barely being on the cusp of consciousness. As you could probably imagine, the beginning stages of my personal meditation journey resulted in a lot of accidental naps, mais c'est la vie!

*   *   *   *   *

In the midst of all of these new experiences, I was granted the deep understanding that there was way more to this current "reality" than we were programmed by society to think. One of the ideas that was really reinforced during my time in high school was eternal, everlasting existence. For all of eternity. Existing forever, ceaselessly. Forever.

When we were younger, my brother was really freaked out by the concept of eternity. So vast and daunting. He used to talk about it with wide eyes, wringing his hands anxiously. And then for a while I was afraid of it too, because it's cool to copy your big brother. But now, as the spiritual expansion train chugs on, the idea makes me feel limitless and inspired. Not to mention curious. Where have I been before this? And where will I go next?

The idea of eternal life was reinforced by my loved ones who had come and gone from the physical plane already. They were still interacting with me in the here and now. Due to my spiritual expansion, I no longer had to rely on my momma as the sole connection between myself and messages received from somewhere simultaneously far away and right here. At this point along my spiritual journey, I gained a deep understanding of the *fact* that loved ones whose physical bodies had died in this current "reality" were still, on the contrary, existing. I felt them with me everyday, in different ways that only became more bold and unquestionable as time and spiritual expansion marched on.

When my mind was somewhere else entirely, from out of the blue I'd receive a quick visual flash of my Grandpa Russell's basement. I'd see the collected beer cans and golf balls lining the walls, surrounding the vintage pool table. I'd get a quick whiff of the smell of his house. One that so uniquely belongs to that space. This quick flash of imagery and sensations would come without me calling to it. Without any form of connecting thought. I took it to mean that my grandpa was near. Other times I'd see a specific tin container. It was cylindrical in shape, cream in color, and decorated with teddy bears. With the lid off, the smell of wax crayons wafted out overwhelmingly. Or I'd remember watching *Mamma Mia* for the first time. Or *Heidi*, while dressed in fleece pajamas cozied up by my grandma. These memories are all so quintessentially associated with my Grandma Halfmann, who passed away my junior year of high school. I often wish I could travel back to those simple memories that made such a positive impact on me. My loved ones bring them to me instead. The nostalgic associations with my grandma and grandpa do not end there. I'm slowly remembering my childhood thanks to them. It's incredible how powerful the little things are. I can recall riding the lawn mower with my grandpa, barefoot and sunburnt. Pretzels on my grandpa's side table while he read the daily newspaper in his recliner. An M&M dispenser, with a dish of pennies always full during my visit. I can recall working in the garden with my grandma. A skip-it that, if I looked away from my feet, never missed the opportunity to knock my ankle. Beautiful hand-made quilts, card games, and county fairs. I felt their love in this "reality" when they stood with me physically, and I'm grateful beyond the capacity of my simple words to feel their love still.

Sometimes I knew they were around because I felt a calming numbness on the left or ride side of my back. I resonated with the left side being my grandma, while the right was my grandpa. At this moment while writing, I can feel my Grandma Halfmann and my Grandpa Russell with me. Along with my Great-Grandma Blohm, whom I never had the chance to meet. I feel their heads near mine, energy buzzing on my back and my shoulders. It's a comforting feeling, which is not typically the feeling that's assumed when recognizing that invisible heads are floating nearby.

The more I acknowledge their presence, the more I feel their energy around me. When I drive in my car, I feel them sitting with me. And when I blast the music and yell out, "let's jam, fam!" I feel their energies singing and dancing along. At the right moments, I even catch quick glimpses of them in the rearview mirror. Remember when I talked about those damn reflective surfaces? Visiting spirits love the rearview mirror. Especially at night. I'll check my mirror quickly, scanning for cars, and be caught off guard to see someone sitting in my backseat for the briefest moment. Here and there in the blink of an eye, naturally.

Feeling the presence of my loved ones became normal. Even our good boy, Scooby Doo, who had passed during this time in my life popped in to say hello every now and again. Relaxed in my bed at night, I'd often feel the familiar heavy hop onto the foot of my bed that lacked any manner of grace or precision. Just Scooby finding his sleepy spot, as he did when he was still physically here. Or sometimes I'd hear a sound that sounded so distinctly like his once annoying whine for treats. Now I smile everytime I hear it. Scooby visits me often in my dreams, as well. He's all over the spiritual place exploring, just like he did in his lifetime here on Earth. He was known as the mayor of the neighborhood where we lived with my dad, for his fondness for the people and his parading through the subdivision. One night I dreamt of him, my momma, and I playing with childlike innocence outside. I threw a stick as far as I could, knowing that he would chase it down but I shouldn't expect him to bring it back. He was never much for the outdated ritual of fetch. Too progressive for that antiquated activity. He zoomed off towards the stick and into the woods where he disappeared. That's when I came into awareness, realizing I was dreaming and that Scooby wasn't here physically anymore. I remember crying, calling out to Scooby to come back, if only for a moment.

"Why didn't we have more time with him?" I cried to my momma, who looked on at my waterworks with a quiet neutrality.

She replied by pointing into the distance and saying, "Look Morgan, he's still with us."

And from the woods Scooby appeared, on a wild sprint back at us. He was youthful in physical appearance and energy. A large contrast to the way he left this lifetime. I spent the rest of the dream knowing that it could end at any minute. Any minute, I'd be waking up in a Scooby deprived world. But instead of focusing on the inevitable, I embraced the unbelievable, the incredible, and I spent a few fading moments running free and living in the present with our good boy. And when I awoke from the dream, I sent a silent "thank you" to Scooby for reaffirming what I already knew deep down. I'd see Scooby again, whether in my memories from the past, my dreams in the coming nights, or someday, somewhere else entirely far better than where we are right now. And the same goes for all of my loved ones, and then some.

  Those very same loved ones come and go, on a different schedule that I'm sure doesn't resemble a schedule at all compared to the likes of mine in this "reality". But they're around every time I need them without fail. I share with them the worries and fears that jump around in my head, and they comfort me by sending me supportive energy and unconditional love. I ask them questions all of the time, and sometimes I receive answers. But not always, because I'm not meant to know everything. That's something that I think my momma gets annoyed with me for; my insatiable appetite for having answers. My grandparents and my momma remind me often that I need to go with the flow, live life as it comes, just be present, exercise freewill, and all that hooplah. What a tease it is sometimes to be surrounded by the means to answers, and to have to "just be present". Just another thing I'm working on.

  Opening up to all of these new equally frightening and exciting abilities and facets of spirituality was made possible by the support of my momma. Her being a role model for what I wanted to become. But it was also thanks to the support team I have beyond this "reality". The ones who see the greater plan unfolding. The ones who patiently wait for this fickle and goofy twenty-some-year-old to figure it out. You know who you are. And trust me, I'm working on it.

♡ Chapter 5 ♡

This Is What Happens When I'm Unsupervised

And suddenly I'm supposed to figure out what I want to do with my life. How did this happen? They all said I had so much time. They were wrong, time really does fly in this current "reality". To quote Smashmouth, "the years start coming and they don't stop coming." But what do we do in times of distress? We persevere. So this section of my life, the conclusion of highschool and beyond, was characterized by vision boards. Great, elaborate displays of my deepest desires. That's really how I got into the university of my dreams, because honestly my personal essay was nothing special. I credit my finely-detailed vision boards for bringing a bunch of other ideas to fruition. But I started using vision boards before I knew of their magical power. I used them before I even knew they had a name.

I have been creating vision boards, and obsessively tweaking them, ever since I was twelve-years-old or so. It's simple really. Find a base, such as a cork board at a thrift store. Cut out some pictures that represent what you want in life from an old magazine that your momma left laying around. Deny any knowledge of the missing magazine when your momma asks. And watch as your reality is created before you, by you, with the magazine clippings, gratitude, and surrender of control. You hold within yourself the ability to create your own reality. And if there's one thing you take from this book, please take that. Save it for a rainy day or contemplate it immediately. You are more powerful than you know. The tools to create are not only around you physically, but within you energetically, innately. As above, so below. As within, so without. You are as powerful as the Universe, for the Universe is within you, just as you're within the Universe. Three quarters of you is the same kind of water that beats rocks to rubble, and all that jazz. With that understanding churning in your head, entertain the idea that every thought or idea within you can be brought to fruition outside of you. It's a law of the Universe, don't @ me. Everything is made up of energy.

We ourselves vibrate ceaselessly at differing frequencies, but we vibrate nonetheless. Our physical bodies, the physical world around us, our thoughts, our words. All dancing at particular frequencies, waiting to be transmuted through intention.

Before I knew of their magic, vision boards were simply creative outlets. Collages that I would hang on my wall and contemplate as though at an art gallery. As much as a twelve-year-old could contemplate aesthetically organized magazine clippings of Zac Efron, flowers, and puppies. I remember in my premier collage I also had a clipping of the Eiffel Tower which stayed on all vision boards that followed in the years to come. My junior year of high school, I traveled to Paris and saw the Eiffel Tower in person, among many other attractions in France that I once only dreamed of. It was sometime after that trip of a lifetime that I noticed the Eiffel Tower on the vision board that was laying on the floor in my room. How curious. As my spiritual journey marched on, the notion of vision boards became increasingly more powerful in my life. I ran with it. And since my discovery of the magic of vision boards, the contemplations and manifestations have become more intentional and more validating.

I've always had a few boards scattered around in various locations. But always making sure that one travels with me. There was one specific vision board that I sat by like an altar, doing my darndest to manifest what the pictures and words foreshadowed. I found the cork board at a Goodwill, desperate for some TLC. I painted the edges steel blue, my favorite color. In the beginning stages of understanding how vision boards actually worked, I only pinned one idea at a time to give it all of my focus. The first idea that I remember putting intention into was my dream of being a captain on my high school soccer team. This was after my trip to France; after realizing how powerful pinning and reflecting on an image everyday, like the Eiffel Tower, truly was. I was in the second semester of my junior year of high school, and it was bold of me to assume that a junior would be voted as a varsity captain when that role was typically reserved for seniors. But I pinned a paper to the board that read:

I will be voted as a captain for the varsity soccer team this season.

I entertained the idea daily. For shits and giggles, as one would say. And although it felt like a far off reach, I envisioned what it would feel like to be a captain. It felt like it was already my experience. So I took inspired action, meaning I busted my butt at practice like a captain would. I embodied the energy of what I desired.

Soon enough it was the day. All of us girls stumbled onto the bleachers on the edge of the soccer field, with our clunky cleats, scraps of paper, and pencils. Our coaches asked us to write down three girls who we'd like to have as our season captains. I voted for three hard-working senior girls who I knew deserved the spots. Others scribbled their votes.

"We'll tally them up while you girls take a lap around both fields," the head coach instructed.

We all groaned in unison but hopped from the bleachers and started dribbling. I really didn't plan on the vision board working, but as you might have guessed, I was selected as one of the team captains. To my utter shock. The coaches sat us back down on the bleachers and read off the names. Two seniors named captains before me, and then…

"The third captain will be Morgan."

How extraordinary. I had just discovered a new powerful tool.

So I hung my vision board(s) up on a wall, and took a small chunk of time everyday to envision myself manifesting all that I had tacked up on them. Over time and through various research, I uncovered important ingredients necessary for manifesting exactly what I desired. The first is gratitude. Being gracious for that which you already have attracts more abundance. Gratitude opens your life up to allow more in, whereas feelings of lack constrict and only attract more lack. That being said, the second ingredient is to focus on feeling the energy of having what you desire, rather than the lack. Embody what you desire to bring to fruition. How does having that item make you feel? What does your day entail as that specific profession? How do you feel in that experience, the experience that is already yours? The Universe is apt to flow with the energy you put out. If you put out the energy and embodiment of your dream job, it *will* come to you when divine timing is right.

The third ingredient is inspired action. Take the necessary, physical steps that lead you closer to your vision. Whether that's by putting in the work at soccer practice or continuing through higher education or so on. We still live in a physical world at the moment, so this is an important part of creating your reality. The fourth ingredient is surrender. Give up control, expectations, and the attachment to a specific unfoldment. Rid yourself of the emotional ties to an outcome, as that's constriction and constriction attracts lack. Surrender is the ultimate form of trust in the Universe; in yourself. The

Universe always provides what we need, and it becomes a whole lot easier if we just allow that to happen without controlling how the outcome unfolds. Focus on what you desire, and trust that it's yours regardless of "how".

The next time I witnessed the unquestionable power of my vision board was senior year of high school. I was looking into schools where I could further my education after graduation. The one that stuck out to me was the University of Wisconsin. Madtown, baby! Oh, the things I could accomplish there seemed limitless in my daydreams. So I applied. I had the grades, test scores, extracurricular activities. All the good that would make me a considerable candidate for admission. The idea of being at the university was a romantic one for me. I envisioned myself moving into my dorm room. I embodied the feelings of a college freshman; excited, curious, nervous, free. I imagined the initial excitement of being in class and meeting new people and joining in on all that college had to offer. It was mine. I could see it just a few months off in the distance.

And because I knew it was mine, I had no emotional ties to the outcome. I was excited, absolutely, but I wasn't worried or stressed or anxious. I was simply allowing what was meant to be, to be. I threw the idea up on my vision board and let what was meant to happen, happen. And soon enough, I received my letter of acceptance. I was a *badger!* And then I saw the tuition costs. Maybe I *wasn't* a badger! In my current financial standings, there was no way I could afford that bill. Every year. For four years. But that's another topic for another book, or political candidate.

I remember being so torn on how to continue, as I'm sure a lot of students are. I wanted that solid education. I worked hard for it. I didn't want the bill. What was a girl to do? Oh yes, I know. I ripped a piece of paper out of my handy-dandy notebook and wrote:

I will not have to worry about my finances for the 2016-2017 school year at UW-Madison!!!

Everyday I would read that scrap of notebook paper with gratitude and surrender on my mind. Gratitude, for the opportunities I've had already that brought me to that point in life and the ones I knew were to come through the university. And surrender, because the Universe works in mysterious ways compared to my fickle human mind. I trusted that. I accepted the admissions offer, discarding all other acceptance letters I had received, knowing that tuition would not be an issue. Where that confidence came from was beyond me at the time. It was beyond my dad, too, who I knew was worried about my naivete.

But as the tuition bill due date was approaching, the money started accumulating. From many different sources, in large amounts and small. Scholarships from the community that I applied for. Financial aid grants. A college fund that my Grandpa and Grandma Russell had saved up for me, to my surprise. Graduation gifts in the form of crisp $20 bills. My own savings from my summer job working at the city park. Would you believe me if I told you at the start of my first semester I had just enough money collected to cover the entire tuition bill for the 2016-2017 year? *Just* enough. The *exact* amount. So please create vision boards. Manifest all that you desire with the best of intentions, all the gratitude you can muster, the confidence that it's already yours, and the cherry on top, surrender. It's a most wonderful type of magic, and the whole world can wield it.

High school graduation came and went. Some of my closest friends gave the most thoughtful speeches, but other than that the ceremony was a drag. High school graduation was something that seemed so monumental building up to it, but once I was sitting in the crowd of students awaiting my diploma, I was really only feeling hungry and bored.

Fast-forward to that following fall. My dad helped me move down to Madtown, channeling his sadness into irritability while we moved all that I over-packed into the tiny dorm room of the aptly nicknamed "shitty Witte Hall".

"Did you really need to pack every book that you own?" my dad dead-panned.

I just shrugged, "That's not *every* book I own…"

Thank you Universe for slowly but surely helping me to uncover and to remember the powerful tools that are within us and all around us, that helped me to create the reality I desired. I had freedom and a surplus of opportunities before me, and I even had my best friend Eva as a roommate for that first year. My curiosity of and desire for spiritual expansion was ever-present. I was waking up more and more everyday.

And at the same time I found myself sleeping a lot. I took a lot of naps that first semester of school, as is the college way. As a freshman, I was stuck with 8am classes. And while I had graduated high school only a few months prior, getting up early to sit through an hour and a half lecture was much more difficult. It's illogical, but I don't make the laws of the Universe. During a short, midday nap on a typical Tuesday afternoon, I gained awareness while flying through the city on the astral plane. I ventured to the university soccer field and saw a game in progress, from the coolest vantage point high in the sky. I saw students walking to and from classes. I heard the cars honking at the students who weren't paying attention while walking to and from classes. Maybe astral traveling was my ticket into exclusive frat parties on campus..

Another time, I fell asleep early in the evening after cranking out a paper. The next thing I knew I was walking up to Eva's house back in Marinette, fully aware. Why did my astral body feel compelled to travel to her house, when Eva was probably passed out in the bunk beneath me? Nevertheless, I remember sitting cross-legged on the front lawn while I looked in the window to see her momma watching a TV show. Do you ever get the feeling that you're being watched? That's me.

My astral experiences happened more and more frequently, based out of that tiny, tiny dorm room. Maybe the newfound freedom of living away from home resonated with my astral body. As with all of my spiritual experiences that couldn't be shared with the typical lecture-hall buddy, I wrote these travels down. Since the beginning, when my momma came clean about the reality of our "reality", I have stayed true in writing everything down. My experiences have taken over the notes section of my phones through the years. I've started more notebooks than I can count or keep track of. And thank God for flash drives because my laptop has run out of space at this point, too.

I wrote all of my experiences down, and one day I had the epiphany to put some order to the disarray of stories that had comprised a colossal part of my life.

"I'm gonna write a book," I whispered to Noah, stationed at a small table on the second floor at a quiet Starbucks. Students were camped out all over the coffee shop sipping venti coffees like their grades depended on it. Noah and I were trying to stay busy studying, but we found ourselves encouraging the procrastinators in each other instead. Noah was likely searching for new film-score playlists to listen to.

"Is it a memoir on being a survivor of the keto diet?" Noah teased.

A sassy remark. How quintessentially Noah. His quick wit was only rivaled by his active listening skills. He listened to my newest idea at full attention as I rambled on about hypotheticals and spontaneous ideas. We brainstormed future possibilities, riling each other up about another one of our ideas that seemed far out but yet so close.

"You should start reaching out to publishing companies, just to get some information or to get your name out there," Noah suggested.

"Alright! I'm gonna do it now!" And my fingers went click-clack, giving my information to the first publishing company that popped up on Google. I hadn't written a word of the book yet, but I felt compelled by the forces of elation to tell that publishing company all about my vision.

Aside from being a passionate and creative outlet, putting this book together was also incredibly therapeutic; cathartic, really. Suddenly there was a purpose behind the experiences I had been collecting on pages. There was a way for me to actively reflect on what I was learning, and release. For the first time in a long time, expression would win over repression. I would connect the experiences and find the inspiration in them, rather than tucking them in my pocket on a scrap piece of paper. Putting the book together would help me to express what I had been hiding for a long time, from the outside world and myself.

"No more running, Morgan. We're gonna figure this out!" quipped my highest and purest self, high-fiving me from some other dimension.

It was only the beginning of remembering and feeling safe to express my true, authentic self. You gotta start somewhere. I decided to start in the upper level of that swanky Starbucks on State Street.

The random publishing company that I gave all of my information to was a motivation on multiple occasions. In the years to come, they always popped in at the perfect moment, as divine timing would have it, to encourage my writing. I remember one day in particular, I was feeling lazy and unmotivated and the works. I briefly debated between adding onto my book or taking a nap. The nap won. So I flopped onto my bed. But no sooner had I made that decision and closed my eyes when my phone started ringing at high volume. I answered it quickly out of confusion only to find out it was the publishing company calling to check in on how the book was coming along. I wasn't particularly forthcoming with the details of my book, considering I really had nothing hearty to share at the time. They got the hint and ended the call with, "keep working on it!" So I took that as a hefty sign from the Universe, and I cranked out a couple thousand words documenting experiences that were only the precipice of my ongoing spiritual journey. I prefaced each new excerpt internally with "maybe someone else can relate to *this* experience!" That's the goal!

In between being a diligent student, working on my book, and experiencing a spiritual journey that was never-ending, I also dabbled in the fine arts of college partying from time to time. That first semester of college was like a movie. Slow motion, packed house parties with questionable wop sloshing from red solo cups. Everyone chanting "keg-stand" like in that one song about college. Frat parties with lists, where you had to know the right people. Pregaming on rooftops by day, chanting in the football field bleachers by night. It was a wild time, accelerated by freedom and vodka sodas. I felt so high that first semester, except for Sunday's, when the hangover would catch up with me. But the low followed, as it is apt to do. I was lowering my frequency with every can of beer I shotgunned. I threw the idea of protecting my frequency to the party gods. The party gods always demand a sacrifice.

It should come as no surprise that alcohol lowers your energetic frequency, considering that alcohol is not wonderful for the health and wellbeing of your physical body. Alcohol desensitizes you to your psychic abilities. So imagine what binge-drinking three or more days of the week would do to someone. It should come as *no surprise* that my frequency declined, along with my mental health.

Remember when I said I did a lot of mid-day napping? It intensified. I couldn't get out of bed. I didn't *want* to get out of bed. Bed was patient. Bed was kind. It was a dark time in my life, though outwardly you would wonder what I had to feel despair about. And like most experiences with dark times, it came when everything was really good. Well, physically good. It came when I was really high. And as though fingers snapped and willed it, I became really low. But it wasn't a pair of metaphorical fingers, it was me and free-will conjuring up a chance to learn another lesson in this physical "reality". A "reality" that is synonymous with a classroom.

Here I was at the school of my dreams, the school that I manifested into my path. But there I was, sleeping through all of my classes. Purposefully missing class after class. Deleting email after email from one irritated teaching assistant. Ordering pizza after pizza from a local favorite that I couldn't afford but yet somehow still managed to afford. The world continued on around me, when I just wanted everything to slow. Maybe even stop for a second or two. Some days were better than others, referring to my energy and motivation levels. On one of these days, I slipped on some sweatpants and carried my backpack down to the first floor lounge area. A change of atmosphere would be good for me, as opposed to the tiny, tiny dorm room with the white brick walls. It was 11 o'clock at night on a Friday, so no one was studying. Those Madison parties are hard to pass up freshman year. I plopped my butt onto a cushy couch in the corner, Criss-crossed legs balancing my laptop and anthropology book. Like a robot, unfeeling and automated, I began copying the vocabulary terms from the anthropology book into my notebook. Writing helps you retain, I told myself. Except I wasn't processing what I was writing. I was only copying the information letter by letter, not able to remember the terms prior once I moved onto the next. Yes, this was learning. I see an A coming my way.

I coped down term after term until the sleepies caught up with me. It seemed to be a pretty uneventful night, aside from the fact that I finally got out of bed and did something. Back to my lofted bed, I went. But nothing is really ever as it seems. Things are always transpiring behind the scene; beyond this "reality" that we see as the only reality. I accomplished more than just a little studying that night in the first-floor lounge of one Shitty Witte Hall.

Before I realized the full extent of what transpired that night, a lot of time passed by. I continued on in the same fashion, laying in bed and avoiding responsibility, until my momma called one day. Momma always knew when things were off. One time a few months earlier I came home from school for the weekend, whereupon I smoked weed for the first time earlier that day.

"You've smoked pot, haven't you?" she pressed.

"No! Absolutely not! I have no connection to the devil's lettuce!"

She only studied me for a minute and walked away.

My mom could tell something was off with me even a couple hundred miles away, and she felt it was her maternal duty to come visit for a weekend. I was excited to give her the tour of the campus I had been avoiding for weeks.

We spent a great deal of our time that weekend holed up in my dorm room streaming *Ghost Adventures* or *The Dead Files*, lights off, curtains drawn, stretched out on the uncomfy futon.

"Should we order a pizza?" my momma asked, barely taking her eyes off of the spooky show.

No chance I'm *not* her daughter.

Eventually we found ourselves bopping down State Street, the area of the city that was monopolized by coffee shops, fruit bowl vendors, trendy and overpriced clothing stores, and gift shops that sold ironic beer themed gifts, primarily. As the Law of Attraction would have it, we found ourselves crossing paths with a spiritual shop, crystals and tapestries decorating the display window. It seemed we had only stepped into the front entrance when I was picking up a pen and signing up for a psychic reading, eyes wide and palms a little sweaty.

The psychic medium that sat before us, Jean Anne, had so much light about her. A couple years into the future, and a few chapters ahead, she makes a second appearance in our lives. But at this point in time we had only just met, squeezed into a tiny black room that was once a bank vault. I love repurposing. The readings commenced. My momma first, and then me. The information Jean Anne provided us was clear and resonating, validation hitting us left and right. But nothing too exciting stood out. Nothing like important life missions or crazy circumstances coming our way. All relatively useful and common information...except at the conclusion of my reading. There was something that puzzled Jean Anne, as foretold by her eyebrows squishing together curiously. She analyzed her astrological tarot cards that had been spread around an astrology board and finally spoke.

"You have a boyfriend," she smiled up at me in relief, like she cracked the code.

My turn for squished eyebrows, "Ha, no…"

"Are you talking to a boy?" she asked, our eyebrows now in a battle of *most confused*.

Again, I answered, "nope!"

"Well then," she concluded, "someone really likes you. There's a boy that I guarantee is going to be coming into your life, if he's not a part of it already. He is pretty much in love with you."

Nice. That's what I like to hear, Jean Anne. I took that information with a grain of salt...and I let it propel me into a heap of hopeless romantic mush for the next few months. I made sure I looked extra cute and cozy when I walked through my dorm building. At coffee shops I tried my best to appear mysterious. Probably just looked confused, honestly. I smiled at everyone. But then again, most people did that so I didn't stand out. Welcome to the midwest! Time went on in a linear fashion as it does in this current "reality", and...nothing.

A few months later, I had another reading done with a different psychic medium. She provided me with accurate and resonating information, until the mystery man was brought up once again.

"Your boyfriend really loves you," she cooed, genuine excitement for me and my flourishing love life.

"What boyfriend? I'm single," I deadpanned.

"Really?" she asked like she was shocked, "Well, then there is a boy that has it bad for you. I think he's someone in your everyday life. Anyone you can think of?"

Lemme scan real quick. "Not one bit, no," I replied. I was stumped, and a bit annoyed. If this guy had it bad for me, then why wasn't he doing something about it? But once again, I took the information and went on my way.

Then it all came to a head one unsuspecting afternoon at a sandwich shop. I walked in for lunch with my momma and my Aunty Tami. As I mentioned earlier, my Aunty Tami is a psychic-medium, just like my momma. In fact, they both began to acknowledge their abilities at the same time. And thus, a power couple was born. They worked in tandem for a few years, providing messages to clients in one-on-one and group settings. Their abilities complemented each other. On top of her psychic and mediumistic abilities, my Aunty Tami is also a certified Reiki master. Reiki is a holistic healing practice in which pure energy is channeled through a Reiki practitioner to the patient. This is typically done by the practitioner running their hands a few inches over the patient's body, pinpointing the location of pains, illnesses, and blockages, and cleansing those areas with divine, healing energy. Beyond her spiritual abilities, my Aunty Tami is a hyper woman, with a "take no shit" demeanor. A powerful being with a genuine heart.

While shoving a delicious ham and cheese hoagie in my face, my Aunty Tami began to read me. It was always a treat when she offered to share a message with me and then consequently snowballed into a full-on reading.

"Do you have a boyfriend?" she questioned.

"No," I snapped, looking to my momma immediately, "but that's funny you ask because multiple readings I've had in the past year have referenced a boy."

"Are you sure? You're not talking to a boy at all? Is there anyone in your life who might have a giant crush on you?" my Aunty Tami pressed.

I just continued chomping on my hoagie. Same questions. Different day. Still very much single at that point.

"I really have no idea, honestly. I've been trying to figure it out for almost a year now."

Then it hit my Aunty Tami. I knew because she jumped in the air and yelled out my name in the tiny sandwich shop.

"Morgan! He's dead!"

Excuse me? I paused in mid-bite of my hoagie.

"He's a spirit that's with you. He has a giant *crush* on you! He's *attached* to you, on your back right now! He's always with you!"

My Aunty Tami was all but high-fiving herself, having cracked the case. On the other hand, I was actively smashing my face against the counter I sat at. I had been on the lookout for the love of my life for months, and turns out he'd literally been piggybacking on me this entire time. What cruel fate! Some Shakespearean work to say the least.

My Aunty Tami focused for a few moments to tune in with the spirit.

"His name is Nick," she explained, "and I can see the moment that he found you and attached himself to you."

I was all ears.

"It was late at night. I see you sitting in a lobby-like area. Your dorm building, I'm assuming. It looks comfy. There are chairs and couches scattered everywhere, and you were sitting on a couch in the corner. You were the only one in the room. I see you copying down terms from a textbook. The class ended in "ology". Was it anthropology? Did you have that for a class this past fall semester?"

She rambled off the vision appearing in her mind's eye, quickly conjuring up the distinct memory from my not too distant past. I nodded, validating what she was seeing. Confirming this big moment with a small gesture.

"Okay, yep, you were copying down terms from your anthropology textbook. The terms were on the sides of the pages. You were writing them down in your notebook, in a bad state of mind, questioning what the point of doing that menial task was. It was as though you were on autopilot. You weren't processing anything. You were just copying down terms one after the other, your mind somewhere else."

Eyes wide and completely entranced by what was transpiring, I continued listening.

"That's when he saw you. You were this bright light in a dark place," she explained.

In retrospect, my light was probably more of a dim glow. But Nicky was still digging the vibe, what can I say.

"I see you picking up a physics book off the ground and checking it out. That's when he attached to you, in that instant. And he likes you. Boy, does he like you a lot," my Aunty Tami started giggling.

"Heh, what's not to like?" I joke to fight off discomfort.

My Aunty Tami continued, "Have you felt creatively blocked lately? Uninspired? Unmotivated? Have you done anything creative recently?"

I thought it over for a minute, "No, I haven't felt *good* in a long time I guess. I haven't done much of anything lately."

She nodded, knowingly.

"Morgan, that's because you have so much dead energy on you. He has unknowingly cut you off from your creativity, your vitality, your liveliness. You've felt really lost and down and dejected, haven't you?"

At this point, my Aunty Tami eased up on the hyper energy. The mood was shifting. We were getting into the heavy part, where she would touch on the very human emotions that were weighing on me. Curses.

"That's how I've felt, yes," I sniffled quietly.

"That's because his energy is mixing with yours. It's consuming you. He's not causing any of this on purpose, but that's what happens when spirits attach themselves to us so strongly, when we're already at low frequencies and vulnerable."

All those weeks locked away in my dorm, I knew the feelings I had been dealing with felt alien. They felt outside of me, while working within me. Talk about a toxic relationship.

After learning about Nick's attachment to me, our relationship started to get serious. I came to notice him with me often in the weeks to come. One night in particular I was visiting home. Just minding my own business, watching some cringey reality TV when I felt all tingly on my back and neck.

"Hello Nick," I smiled.

Nick followed me everywhere around the house, particularly in the evening when our connection was stronger. I could feel him on my back, and almost faintly see him marching in tow behind me. This was so silly. I hadn't experienced this before. And so, as I do in those situations, I ran into my momma's room to share. Nick kept up, and my momma noticed him immediately.

"I can see Nick right behind you!" she laughed.

This resulted in me goofily sprinting from wall to wall in her room, around the bed and back and forth through the hallway, seeing if Nick could keep up. We were racing on different planes, through two different dimensions, at evenly matched speeds. Shortly I was breathless from laughter with my abs screaming at me to cease. The best kind of exercise. I was breathless from laughing at the excitement and the absurdity, and so was my momma. I like to think Nick might have been experiencing the same elated feeling. On top of the ridiculousness of knowing that I couldn't shake Nick during my sprints, the connection had me feeling as though my neck was constantly being tickled. My neck crinkled up in defense for a half hour before I could relax. At that point, I superman'd next to my momma, face down into the cushy comforter. We recognized that Nick popped a squat at the foot of the bed.

I looked at my momma, who was connecting to Nick with ease at the moment.

"Why hasn't he crossed over?" I questioned.

A moment passed, "He wants to connect with his loved ones. He wants to make sure they're okay and able to move past his passing."

My momma continued on, but directed at Nick.

"Nick, you need to bring your family to us if you want to communicate with them. We can't reach out to them ourselves. That's not our place."

As we continued to wind down, so did the energy in the room. It felt lighter all of a sudden.

"He left, didn't he?" I asked my momma.

"Yes, I think he's actually sleeping in your bed downstairs," she replied, her eyes positioned up and to the left like she was working to sense him. At that point in time when I visited home on the weekends, I made the executive decision to sleep in a spare bedroom upstairs as spirits were constantly overwhelming me down in the basement bedroom.

"He's sleeping in my bed downstairs?" I chuckled, amused.

My momma chuckled, "'Well' he says, 'where else am I supposed to sleep? It's not like you're sleeping down here.'"

Touché, Nick, you sassy-pants.

But that lighthearted interaction was actually a pivotal moment for me. Nick was helping me to see how misguided I had been about spirits or ghosts. They are just like us living ding-dongs. Only a metaphorical moment ago they *were* living ding-dongs. Spirits that are still connected to this physical plane often want the same things that we do. Understanding, validation, comfort, connection, and so much more. Whether that's a bed to sleep in or the simple acknowledgement of their presence.

After that night and that pivotal realization, I had many heartfelt conversations with Nick, along with the occasional light and goofy conversation. I'd talk with him about everything under the sun really, and he had no choice. It was like I had an imaginary friend in my young adulthood. Perhaps imaginary friends are always people like Nick; the best of company. Or maybe sometimes they're evil old-timey children. But I'll let scary movie directors and future-potential-mother-Morgan worry about that possibility.

Around that same time period, my momma and I took a day trip filled with shopping and good food. One the ride home, a car zoomed past us with a rear license plate reading *SUE*. My momma pointed it out to me.

"I have a spirit hanging around lately named Sue and she keeps sending me signs everywhere. License plate, exhibit A."

"I haven't felt any signs from Nick in a while. C'mon buddy, send me a lil sign," I taunted, calling out to Nicky from the passenger seat of the car.

Nick was on the ball, because it wasn't even two minutes later when we passed a car with a license plate that read *WITTE*, the name of the dorm I lived in. The setting for the beginning of our story. *Witte* was a term I hadn't ever heard until living in that dorm in Madison, so it was bizarre to see it scribed into a license plate back in my hometown. Bizarre, but not entirely surprising. Nick made it happen because we were tight.

As time passed on in that linear fashion things changed, but Nick remained. And that became a problem. For me, because dead energy really is a thing, and only being at the precipice of my spiritual journey I wasn't entirely disciplined in protecting myself energetically. And for Nick, because he deserved a lasting peace that wasn't solely tied to our chaotic-good household. One night as I sat in my bedroom, knowing that he was nearby, I had a heart to heart with him. It went something like this:

"Nick, I have something to say and don't interrupt me."

Haha. Developing-medium humor.

"We've had a fun run. Sometimes literally running, other times immobile. But I think it's time for you to go. And I think you know that too. You have the opportunity to be someplace far better than here. Take it, man. Where you're headed, you'll see loved ones that you didn't even realize you had. They'll be waiting for you. They *are* waiting for you. There'll be so much love and light and peace, and you deserve that. Don't be scared. Be excited. I can't wait for the day that I can return, because I can feel that deep yearning within me. But it's not my time yet. It is yours though, if you're ready. Thank you for being a friend, for teaching me so many things on purpose and by accident. This has been an experience worth writing about, that's for sure. I'll be seeing you someday, and I'll be expecting to meet up when I get back. Let your soul let it in. Let the light envelope every part of you. Remember in this moment how full of love and light you are."

This message that started in my heart and tumbled from my lips felt natural. Powerful. Capable of causing a shift. And a shift did transpire moments after the one-sided conversation. A few tiny tears even slipped down my cheeks amidst it all, because I believed in my words so strongly. I think Nick believed them too, because the energy shift felt a lot like a lack of Nick and a surplus of light. I laid at the foot of my bed, meditating on the feeling of the space around me until I dozed off.

That night I dreamt of Nick.

The dream offered perfect clarity and complete awareness. And for the first time, I had a clear image of Nicky. I dreamt that I was in my dorm room, sitting on my uncomfy futon all alone when the door opened and in he walked. I knew it was him immediately, though I had never developed a mental image of his physical appearance in all the time we spent together. What a terrible girlfriend I was. He sat next to me. We must have talked about trivial, unmemorable things and stuff. The conversations were foggy when I woke up. But who knows, maybe he confirmed some of my strangest questions about existence. The Universe and my higher self probably sensed that part to keep my very physical, human head from exploding in the current now. But I do remember what I could see. And what I saw was a boy, tall and lanky, with dark hair and a gentle demeanor. One of his hands reached out to hold one of mine. Him, light and ethereal and all kinds of other words that describe those above and beyond us. We were two individuals being pulled in different directions, yet sharing an understanding that our connection would continue to exist. Soon enough Nick was pulled one way, and I the other. Him to somewhere far better, and me back to this "reality" that I still needed to experience. But before our time was up, Nick delicately kissed my cheek and whispered, "goodbye, Morgan". That's when I woke up, curled tight on the foot of my bed.

Goodbye Nick and good luck to every boy after Nick because I have rightly placed him high in the sky where he shall remain.

Since that night, Nick has only popped in with little hello's every great once in a while. It's my greatest hope in the matter and my current understanding that he passed on that night. He has to be somewhere far better, because as I was writing this section, sharing about that good boy, he provided me with a beautiful sign. I felt his energy around me while in the thick of detailing this story, so I spoke to him a bit.

"Thank you, Nick, for everything you taught me. For giving me that experience, and for being a friend. Where are you now? Someplace wonderfully beyond my understanding, I bet."

Immediately after I whispered these words, the music I had been playing through my laptop switched in the middle of a song. The song that started playing unrequested when I checked Spotify was titled *Heaven*.

I'm spoiled when it comes to receiving validation, but I'm even more spoiled when it comes to the beautiful souls that I've had the honor of experiencing this current "reality" with. So thank you, Nick. I'll be seeing you.

After Nick moved on, I realized that I needed to make a change to my current situation. Everything felt all wrong. Nothing was easy. Nothing was exciting. Nothing made me feel alive. And that was no way to exist. This physical "reality" is too negative and heavy already to not actively chase what sets your soul on fire. And taking taxing courses that did not reflect my true passions was constantly extinguishing all the passion that I had inside me.

To preface, I have been experiencing signs for years at this point, though it took me a while to give them the time of day that they deserved; to acknowledge that they were actually messages and not just coincidences that my delicate brain concocted.

On a Friday afternoon I spontaneously packed a bag and hopped on the bus that would take me home, up north, for the weekend. Sunglasses on with my hood up, headphones in. Hidden in the furthest seat back on the coach bus. Arms crossed, backpack taking up residence in the seat next to me. Not interested in any kind of communication, if my body language wasn't clear. And it should have been clear; I took a semester of a nonverbal communication course.

If you had access to my thoughts, you would have heard a civil war actively transpiring between social-appearance and my soul's desire. I wanted to leave Madison. I wanted a fresh start. I wanted to feel excited about my current now, and not just dream about the future that may or may not come. A curious idea had been swirling through my head that it was my sovereign right, perhaps even obligation, to be happy. Or at least to create a reality that resonated with the deepest parts of me. And while at one point Madison did resonate, the time came and went. I like to think that I experienced what I needed to experience, and now my soul was ready to move onto something brand new. Stat. The sun was setting on my time at Madison. Which could only mean that the sun would soon rise on an entirely new experience.

But here I was, hidden in the back of the bus behind a hood and sunglasses. A spectator to the onslaught that was happening inside my head. Who would win? Social appearance called in it's ally, practicality. My soul's desire was outnumbered, but still strong and passionate.

In a separate, less violent region of my brain, I was simultaneously contemplating switching to online school. But I was a perfectionist and at the time I cared too much about what people thought and I didn't want to let anyone down, and the list of ego-driven thoughts went on. I really had to sit on this bus for four hours and contemplate my future? Had I died and gone to hell?

Music will save me. I scrambled for my headphones, quickly hitting shuffle on a random playlist. The thoughts would not cease. Head, meet window! And it's as if that collision of my head against the window inspired a divine message.

"*Listen,*" I heard somewhere deep in my random thoughts.

The civil war came to a silent standstill, soldiers at attention. In that short moment, I listened to the lyrics that were being sung and heard, "Remember you're still free to make the choice and leave". I scoffed at the sky, and at Ed Sheeran, but closed my phone to see the time 5:55pm staring back at me.

Numbers hold a great deal of symbolism, or so numerology would have us believe. Which I do believe. Whenever I see a triple digit, repeating number such as 555, I reflect on what my thoughts sounded like at that moment or what my current situation was. I've been taught that if my thoughts were positive at the time, they were being reinforced by the Universe. If my thoughts were negative, I needed to switch my frame of mind and find the positive. Each number has a different spiritual meaning. I am still doing personal research to understand which meanings resonate with me for each number, so I encourage you to research numerology in your spare time and create your own understandings. When I looked up the number five, it spoke of life changes. How fitting. How absolutely fitting, Universe. Maybe that experience doesn't sound monumental to you, but in that moment I started shedding the dark and dismal "protective" barrier that I was wearing 24/7. That moment inspired an unraveling inside me. Feelings of excitement began to surface faster than feelings of fear. Wonder and whimsy took precedence over insecurity and shame, contemplating on the path I could create in this current "reality". I focused on what possibilities lay ahead, rather than focusing on what I'd be leaving behind or what was holding me back. Of course I didn't flip a switch all at once. But a shift had occurred, courtesy of a sign from the Universe in the form of an Ed Sheeran song. I believed in myself and my path again, and I made the decision that resonated most with my soul. A few short weeks later, I switched from the University of Wisconsin to online courses that would unknowingly act as the perfect catalyst for future Morgan. Yes, practicality and social-appearance won many battles, but my soul's desire won the war. I hope history really does repeat itself. For me. For you. For the collective.

From that moment on, and even before though in hindsight I could have given them more attention, signs have been given to me plentifully. That surplus of signs only increased as I continued to acknowledge them. I even learned after a while that I could harness the ability to bring forth signs all on my own. Today, I know when I'm spitting truth because I'll get goosebumps. Whenever I need reassurance that what I believe to be the truth is in fact the truth, I'll speak what I believe and wait to be confirmed by goosebumps. It's like I'm offering poetry and my loved ones, spirit guides, and angels are all snapping their fingers back at me. By acknowledging these "coincidences", or synchronistic events that seem to resonate with my life, I only began to notice more and more.

Signs from loved ones and the Universe come in all shapes and sizes, and definitely at times that we least expect them. They're dropped on us in the form of feathers, they stop us in our tracks as pennies, and sometimes they even pop a squat on a bench beside us. I experienced an enlightening and humbling sign one normal day that I still think about often. It came shortly after I switched to online school. Though I knew I had the Universe on my side, I felt fearful of my future, resentment for my past, and hopelessness from day to day. The triad of negativity. At the time, I had been working as a nanny while living down in Madison in an apartment with my besties. To get to and from the house, I'd either walk, ride my bike, or hop on the bus. Walking was the mode of transportation I frequented, for the exercise and to avoid a $4 bus fee. But once it started to get dark out earlier, I felt more justified taking the twenty-minute bus ride compared to the forty-minute walk. Biking was a last resort. The hills along the path were ruthless.

On this particular night, it was already dark out when I was able to take off from the house I watched over. It was only ten minutes to the nearest bus stop, but I walked it slowly knowing that I had a while until the next bus rolled around. The neighborhood I passed through morphed from elaborately constructed houses adorned with big windows facing Lake Monona, into an area of the city that was less outwardly glamorous. Litter and potholes a-plenty. The bus stop that I neared had one of those eerie lights atop it. You know, the kind that flickers every so often, casting a SYFY yellow onto a small vicinity. I sat for a bit on the bench inside the partial enclosure, frequently checking my phone for the time. Still fifteen minutes before the next bus would arrive. Typically those minutes would take forever to pass, considering the cool December night. But as is usually the case when I'm least expecting it, a sign from the Universe ambled my way.

An old woman popped a squat on the bench beside me, safe from the cool winds that were blowing. Like I do when any stranger is in close proximity, threatening to interact, I began to gauge the woman for her energy. She felt light and peaceful and good, and all other terms that are synonymous with love.

She turned to me and said, "Merry Christmas sweetie. Or happy holidays. Whichever, but God bless you."

I smiled back, and kindly offered the same greetings and well wishes back at her. It prompted a deep conversation that started with the weather, and led into her sharing her life story with me. In the short time that I had the pleasure of talking with her at that bus stop, I learned a number of things. Her father had come from Jamaica, bringing her family to live in Madison, Wisconsin for a long while. Throughout her life, she traveled to many places in search of a home. Eventually she ended up in Milwaukee, Wisconsin on her own. The apartment complex she lived in had recently experienced multiple break-ins, and because of the increasing amount of trouble, all residents were being made to vacate. This left the woman homeless. She traveled back to Madison where she had a few friends, and spent most of her nights couch surfing or at homeless shelters. She explained that she had just been out shopping for a Christmas present for her godson. From a plastic shopping bag on her lap, she pulled out a pair of pajama pants for me to inspect. She went on to explain that she was debating between going back to her current place of residence for the night, as she was tired, or taking the bus across the entire city and dropping off the present. From frequenting the bus myself, I knew that ride would be over an hour and a half.

"You know what?" she began, "I have other days to be selfish. I'm gonna drop the pajamas off and make his night."

She continued on, telling me that she planned to start setting up hair-cuts for the homeless on street corners.

"I went to beauty school, you know. I could paint their nails, too. It always feels nice to feel beautiful and to be taken care of."

Struck by everything she told me, at a loss for words after being humbled down to nothing, I could only say, "God bless you."

"God bless you too, sweetie. God bless all of us. The world is a dark place right now, but it doesn't have to be that way."

We sat in the silence that followed for a minute or two. I let everything sink in and stew.

And eventually the bus rolled around. We both hopped on, and found seats next to each other. The bus was quiet at the late hour, so I took the peaceful opportunity to absorb everything I had just heard… and I heard a lot. Before she stood up at her stop, the woman leaned in close to me like she was sharing a secret.

"Keep your eyes open. I think we'll be seeing each other again. Good people tend to attract good people."

All I could manage was a wide smile back. I believe I'll see her again someday, somewhere, should the Law of Attraction allow it. After she left, I burrowed into my head for the rest of the ride.

What I realized from that encounter was that every time I was faced with an obstacle, or something that seemed to bring me down, I was presented with a sign that brought me back. They're always being given to us, we just have to accept them. This particular sign reminded me that not only are my problems miniscule in the grand scheme of this "reality", but also that they're not permanent; they don't define me. One thing that really affected my mental stability at that time in life was trying to determine my future living situation. I didn't know whether I was meant to stay in Madison or move back home, and it stressed the hell out of me. But how ridiculous of me to worry when I knew, regardless of where, that I'd have a place to return to at the end of the night. And after this encounter I realized that, regardless of where I am, I could still live my best life. Even though this woman was homeless, she was still choosing to be kind, loving, and selfless. She was giving even though she didn't know where she'd be staying tomorrow or the day after that. She reminded me that regardless of where you're at in your life, you can still choose to be good to others. To give and to serve and to be grateful. And I think that's the secret to abundance. I just hope she knows that she can take those selfish-days and choose to drop the present off some other time. Just as we can choose to be good to others, we deserve the same from ourselves.

These thoughts began to slow down in my head, allowing me to zone back into the present moment. Just in time to pull the cord and hop off at my stop, whereupon I checked my phone to see 5:55pm. Now you should know by now that I'm no rookie when it comes to recognizing signs. The number 555 spoke of life changes and life purpose. How absolutely fitting. I was actively and constantly connecting to my life purpose in the physical and the spiritual, through experiences with compassion, trust, gratitude, and love. And that night was just a wonderful reminder of what this is all about! I shoved my phone back into my pocket and all but skipped back to my apartment with Christmas lights twinkling down State Street and a light of my own expanding within and all around me. How festive.

Signs come to us when we least expect them but when they can have the greatest impact on our direction and expansion. What a beautiful *present* that is. Maybe someone, somewhere took time out of their day to ride the city bus down the entire line to deliver that present and make your night. Or maybe none of this is real and we're all just characters in a video game, being controlled by a kid named Tanner sipping on his sixth Dr. Pepper. You decide.

♡ Chapter 6 ♡

Dancing w/ the Devil to Summer Hits of the 2000's

For a short while I remained in Madison with my friends and the freedom and the frat parties. And still it seemed that I had a strong conscious connection to the Universe, per all of the phenomena that I continuously experienced. But it was a conscious connection that I eventually realized was based out of fearfulness, rather than love. Living in a state of fearfulness can be characterized by any or all negative emotions; jealousy, anxiety, worry, discontent, sadness to name a few. These feelings and more stem from fear, and are therefore disconnected from love and light. So within this state that I put myself in, I was actively creating my reality with fear as the foundation.

I attracted a great deal of fearful experiences during that time period. All experiences that provided me with lessons that my soul needed to learn, but it was like taking the hard way as opposed to a much easier path. At the time I was so oblivious.

"I'm a good person who loves others so deeply. I empathise and want to help others in any capacity!" I would shout from the rooftops of the frat houses.

"Yes, but you need to love and help *yourself*, you goofball!" the Universe would shout back. But I couldn't hear. The advice was drowned out by Fettywap or Kesha blasting from a speaker.

My higher self knew the next step. It seemed that the only way to wrap my fickle human head around the importance of this lesson along my spiritual journey, taking care of and protecting myself, was to break me down until I finally decided to build myself up. Of course, in the most loving way possible. And that's exactly what happened in the months to come.

*   *   *   *   *

Most of the time I didn't realize I was receiving quick glimpses into the future, since it was so ingrained in my brain to blame what didn't immediately resonate on my imagination. I learned that I would do well to follow my intuition, although that lesson hasn't completely stuck the landing yet. One random night, though I'm sure it wasn't random for the burglars, our downtown Madison apartment was broken into. And while I received help in the form of a prophetic dream, it went right over my head. In my dream, I was inside a house. And simple enough, a man was trying to get inside. That was the gist. I knew I didn't want the man inside the house, and I also knew that he really wanted to get in, as is a burglar's disposition. I remember running around the house locking windows and doors, but he was still a threat. In an instant, I realized I was dreaming. Then I woke up. Revisiting that dream after the real-life break-in makes me feel like a total and complete fool for not recognizing the massive sign that was carefully placed inside my dreamstate.

  I remember laying in my sleepiness, curious about the dream but obviously not *that* curious! A few moments passed by as I snuggled deeper into my comforter, comfy-cozy and undisturbed. Then my doorknob twisted open quietly. But as it was an old house, "quietly" was a matter of perspective. I heard the door pop open a smidge, the sound of the bottom sliding over the carpet in my room. So I popped open my eyes. The thing is, my door doesn't just open when wind passes through or what have you. It was latched shut, and the thick carpet floors in my room prevented easy movement. But like I said, I was a *total and complete fool*, so this understanding of the way my door worked was of no importance to me. I was about to enter into a REM cycle, I did not have time for *reason*.

  In my sleepy stupor, I got up and shut the door without investigating which became my second mistake. Door, meet latch. Face, meet pillow. I plopped back into bed with my lamp still illuminating the room, doing its job keeping the low-vibration experiences away while I tried to sleep. Back under the covers I slipped, falling half-asleep. But only half-asleep, thankfully, because minutes later a squeaky tampering noise came from my window. To create a mental image for you, my bedroom window was about three feet away from another building, which created a narrow alley between the two apartment houses. No one ever walked through it so I always had my window open with a screen on to let in fresh air. Additionally, the window was high up off the ground, so you'd need a boost to get a good peek inside.

Those were definitely noises that bordered on suspicious, so I laid there immobile and alert. And if you thought my natural threat response was flight, then you were wrong. When the noise persisted, I popped up off the bed and jumped to my window where I saw a man's face looking in my room. Which one of us was more scared? I probably looked wild. The man immediately jumped down from his grasp on the window and took off sprinting through the alley. In my 2am frazzled state, I ran out to my roommate, Jake, who was pulling an all-nighter studying for an upcoming exam. He had spent most of the night in the living room with papers scattered all around, but I found him in his bedroom taking a short power nap with headphones on.

"Jake, some guy was just peeping in my window!" I cried, grossed out.

"People walk through that alley when they're drunk, I'm sure he was just passing through," Jake offered as a plausible reason, trying to console me.

I deadpanned, "No! He climbed up to my window and when I looked out at him he ran off down the alley."

"Want to sleep in my room tonight?" Jake suggested, "I'll be up studying the rest of the night, you can have my bed. Here, let's hangout in the living room for a bit."

We stumbled back into the living room, planning to have a bit of tea or maybe a whole pot of noodles. Jake's love language is cooking for others, and I too speak the love language of food. But as we stepped back into the living room, things.. felt.. off. We looked at each other briefly, silently communicating our confusion.

"Did you move my stuff?" Jake asked, motioning to a pile of things on the couch by the window. A pile of valuables stacked in an efficient little get-away pile.

Then we both noticed the open window, with the screen ripped out. We made eye contact again, his eyes as wide as mine. We were frozen for a few moments, silently waiting for something to happen. Bracing. When nothing crashed or grabbed us or darted through the house, our words came back.

"Someone was in the house," I thoughtfully suggested.

"Yes," Jake thoughtfully replied.

"Is someone still here?" I questioned, trepidatiously lowering my voice.

Jake ran into his room quickly and returned with two trekking poles, handing one to me and keeping one for himself.

"Take this, we're gonna check all the rooms and wake Hannah up."

Hannah was asleep in the back bedroom with her boyfriend. Not for long! We started calling their phones to discreetly wake them. And when that didn't work, we started yelling Hannah's name from the opposite end of the house. There were a lot of doors and rooms down the hallway. A burglar could have hid in any one of those dark doorways, waiting for innocent students with weak trekking poles to pass by. Eventually we were able to wake the two sleepyheads. And once we had more backup, stationed on each end of the apartment, we checked the rooms off of that dark hallway. Nothing. But we didn't check Noah's room, as the door was closed and the lightswitch for his dark, dark room was in a spot that would leave us vulnerable to a burglar, ready to attack. Noah wasn't home that night, but rushed home when he heard of the excitement.

Jake had originally been studying in the living room, and had moved into his room ten minutes before the incident transpired. Within that ten minutes the burglars had enough time to break into our apartment through our living room window. I'm sure you can guess what happened. Expensive stuff was stolen, cops were called, statements were given. The cops searched the whole house, including Noah's bedroom, and only found one large dirty laundry monster in the corner of his room. No burglar. I stayed up the rest of the night accompanied by my anxiety. I remembered the dream I had woken up from. Although everyone was safe, which was the main concern, my intuition was shaking its fist at me. I wish I could tame my clairvoyant abilities enough to see if Jake gets his Wii-switch returned back to him in the future or if Hannah gets her Beats Pill speaker. Sadly, I have a feeling that's not going to happen.

*   *   *   *   *

The uninvited-type showed up in my meditations too. I was deep into my carefully concocted meditation process, sitting aboard the Hogwarts Express staring out the window when a tall man walked in and sat directly across from me. His energy freaked me out. I knew this right away.

"I don't like you," I blurted.

He didn't answer, but simply remained seated with impeccable posture. He was dressed in a dark suit, and seemed to be in his fifties with salt and pepper colored hair. One particular thought kept churning in my head: *"This guy is the devil."*

"You are not welcome here," I said with a little more impact behind my words. And with that, the man stood up and walked out. I was frazzled by his energy, and the fact that I kept hearing that he was the devil. Was it me conjuring up that thought in my head? Was it him placing the thought in my head, trying to intimidate me? Was he really the devil? I thought he'd be more attractive, enticing. But he was gone, so I regrouped and refocused. My attention went back to the window, watching as we rolled through the calm countryside. But my attention was interrupted again. The salt and pepper haired devil dude, back from the dead, walked in and sat directly across from me once more. He said nothing, only staring at me with his piercing eyes. I did not like him, that much I knew. But this time I sat with his presence and my curiosity, making no sudden movements. Why was he allowed in, in the first place? My spirit guides, guardian angels, and loved ones were the gatekeepers and they knew the stipulations. Of the light, meaning me no harm, etc. Curiosity waning, I once again told him to leave.

"Get out. I don't like you," I said right to his face, channeling a bluntness that I do not typically possess. This time he didn't leave. Feeling really uncomfortable, I said meditation be damned and opened my eyes. I was laying in my bed, and was taken off guard when I saw the same man standing at the foot of it. He was only there for a fraction of a second before he was gone, but it sent me scurrying from my bedroom and kept me out of my apartment for a few hours.

I attempted to find comfort for a while by blending into the mass hoard of students in the campus square. But there I was, wild-eyed and fuming, chaotic-good but angry, stumbling haphazardly, wondering why I was so vulnerable to these beings that felt threatening. How do I keep them out of my head? How do I keep them out of my *room*? I huffed and puffed for another few weeks as similar experiences continued to transpire, per the Law of Attraction. And then my frequency reached an all time low. I was spiraling. *Spiraling*!

I had been home from school following a very wild and scandalous spring break in Florida. I spent most of my time back in my hometown with my best friend and a boy I had been dating. One night my boyfriend took me to a local diner to get late-night coffee with him and his friend. He wanted his friend to share stories from road-tripping across the United States and I, being a Sagitarrius, was enamored by the idea of road tripping and excited to meet a fellow free spirit. Our night was made up of many cups of coffee and numerous stories shared. Fast-forward a couple days and my hometown was getting hit with the most snow we had seen in ages. Everything was shut down on this particular day because the plows could not keep up with the heavy snow. My boyfriend, his bestie, and I decided to go gas-station coffee hopping, since they were the only places open. In hindsight it was ridiculous that we were out on the roads, but hey, we're from the northeast of Wisconsin. We packed into my boyfriend's truck and taste-tested a couple places around town, on a quest to determine the best gas-station coffee in the area. We ended back at my boyfriend's house, us three stationed around the living room with *That 70s Show* playing on the TV in the background. All was normal and as it should be. The boys were in the middle of their own conversation, and I was sucked into Hyde's agenda to stick it to the man.

But out of nowhere, I started to feel *off*. A feeling that I had only experienced in passing moments, and didn't understand yet at this point in space and time. It was like I wasn't alone in my head. Beyond that, it was like I wasn't fully *in control* of my head, or my reality. Things felt shifted, not real. This feeling transformed into intense paranoia the more I focused in on it. I felt pulled to an area of the room, so I tuned in, allowing myself to flow.

Terrified, but allowing for the moment nonetheless.

The room slowed down around me. I zoned all of the stimuli out. I was focused on my boyfriend's friend. Not him, but behind him, in the corner of the room. I'm sure my staring must have made him a little uncomfortable, but nevertheless she persisted. In the corner of the room, playing metaphysical peek-a-boo with me was a being that appeared so vividly in my mind's eye. Internally I was heavy-breathing. Externally I was immobile, eyes unblinking, trying to be as still as possible like I was prey playing dead in the midst of an apex predator. Yes it was all very dramatic and scary in my head at that moment, but the live studio audience from the TV continued on with their scripted laughter like nothing was happening.

"You okay, Morgan?" my boyfriend questioned, picking up on my dissociation.

"Yup, fine," I offered eloquently. I didn't have much more to offer than that at the moment. I had no idea what was going on. This energy that I was among was disturbing my thoughts, causing me to struggle with comprehension and clarity. I had no words to share, as though that part of my brain was failing me. It was an intense overwhelm of my senses and, in hindsight, a lack of knowing what to do with the energy I was experiencing. In my head I called out to my angels and spirit guides, loved ones and my highest and purest self to surround and fill me with the white light, as I felt extremely uncomfortable and and definitely threatened by this new experience.

It wasn't with my physical eyes that I saw this being, but with my third eye; my mind's eye. I held a mental picture of the being, as clear to me as the two boys sitting in the room, who were oblivious to the metaphysical parley that was happening. The being appeared in my mind standing on the opposite side of the room, staring back at me with an energy that felt like malice.

Assert yourself, I thought.

"I don't like you," I sent in its direction. In retaliation, the being came to me, up close and personal. It was hateful. That was the frequency it was vibrating at. So why was it in my experience? I definitely wasn't vibrating with the frequency of hate. Its face was in front of mine, showing me its teeth. Not a smile, but more like a sneer. And then it showed me it growling, nipping at me like an enraged dog. Was I making this up now? No, the very real fear in my physical body said otherwise. At this point in time, I had no idea how to empower myself spiritually. The best I could do was to call to my soul team of spirit guides, guardian angels, loved ones, my highest self, and other multidimensional beings of peace, light, and love. I knew enough to trust that I was safe; that even though I was frightened and experiencing something very new, I was untouchable. Morgan: 1. Threatening being: 0.

I threw my hand in the air, calling on the light to help me shoo this being away. It disappeared from my mind's eye where it stood directly in front of me, but I felt it was still near. The rest of the night was a rather uncomfortable game of hide and seek where I was always the one seeking. I could feel that the being was still around, but I had no understanding of why. And what was it? Or who? All the interrogatives, basically.

It took me a while to finally be able to relax again that night, as every few minutes I'd feel the being somewhere else, lurking nearby. I'd catch a quick glimpse of it standing in various spots around the room. When I could no longer entertain the game we were playing, I tried an idea that popped in my head. Between my hands, I intended to mold a ball of energy, formed from my purest intentions, from a place of love and light. I molded the energy just as someone would mold a ball of clay, except of course the energy was considerably less dense. My hands buzzed, and I could feel the pressure of the energy increasing. I allowed the energy to expand as I collected more, and built upon it. And when it was big and bright and powerful in my mind's eye, I threw it into the middle of the room with the intention to raise the frequency and drive away anything that couldn't hang. Expand, my baby, expand! As the light enveloped the room, I felt the discomfort dissipating. I was eventually able to focus back on the conversation the boys were having, and even chime in with thoughtful responses like a normal person.

The next day, I bopped out of my boyfriend's house real quick and recounted everything to my momma. She could pick up the being, who had apparently hitched a ride with me, right away. We compared what we saw, which was one of my favorite things to do. Validation was always a sweet feeling in the midst of growing into my abilities.

"It has grey-blue skin," I started.

"And little sharp teeth!" my momma added.

"It's not much taller than me. And it makes me think of that Nosferatu guy?" I laughed, unsure.

"But child-like. It looks kind of scrawny," my mom observed.

"Exactly. A scrawny, child-like Nosferatu," I concluded, "So who or what, and why?" I deadpanned to my mom, to the Universe, to Nosferatu standing over in the corner.

Together, my mom and I contemplated what the being was. It obviously didn't appear as a human, dead or alive. Was it truly a malevolent being like it wanted me to think or just misunderstood and succumbing to a very low-vibrational experience? Were we meant to know what the being was, or simply meant to experience it? We'd never experienced one of those guys before. We hadn't the experience to determine what the entity was. So we continued on to see how else it would interact with us or present itself.

The being remained over the next few days, bothering both me and my momma. Typically it remained only as a feeling in our energy field, but at unsuspecting times it appeared in our mind's eye.

"I felt it approach me when I was cleaning," my mom began, "and immediately I told it that it was not welcome if it meant any harm. Well, then it lunged at me and hissed in my face," my momma scoffed. "So I shooed it away with my hand and called on my loved ones to help me dismiss it. It put up a short fight but left pretty soon after. Not good at all, pean."

The next day I left for Madison, headed to my apartment and my friendos. It was time to get back to reality after an eventful spring break, and that meant focusing on schoolwork again. I knew this entity would follow me, but I underestimated its ability to affect me. So I hopped on the bus back to the city, a pep in my step at the though of being back in Madtown. Three hours later and I was lugging my backpack from the bus stop to my bedroom on Gilman Street. The daytime didn't present any obstacles for me. Maybe I was too caught up in seeing some of my favorite people, unpacking, and eating really yummy spicy dumplings from a local joint a few blocks over. Oh but the night, lemme tell you. What a totally different experience. Around 11pm, I barricaded myself inside my bedroom, with the door locked and all of my lights on. Before I did this, I had been out in the kitchen with my roommate, Jake. We were having a normal conversation about what he had going on in the coming week, and then I felt a little off. A little off, like the first time. The intense paranoia was setting in, encouraging me to distrust my surroundings. Things didn't feel real. I felt I was in danger. I felt confused. I felt a lot of unexplainable beliefs. I lost focus of the conversation I was in, only knowing that I didn't feel safe, or fully in control of my head, as though I was in a trance. The being was trying to connect, but it frightened me.

"STOP!" I yelled with the voice inside my head. But little Nosferatu continued. My reality felt distorted. I couldn't look at Jake, because if I did, I felt I would see the being smiling back at me. I looked over to Noah, who was sitting on the couch, and felt unsure of him as well. When Hannah walked in the door a moment later, I felt overwhelmed and outnumbered.

"These are not your thoughts, Morgan. Knock it off. Relax," I rambled internally, attempting to soothe myself.

Everything, I was able to calmly and naturally phase out of the conversation with Jake and retreat at a hasty pace to my bedroom. I locked my door immediately. Then, I made sure music was drowning everything out, lights were illuminating all corners, blankets were covering me, and candles were burning. I had covered just about every one of the senses in hopes of being able to block out the fearful feeling that this being encouraged in me. Around 1am I began to feel better. That's around the same time that Noah texted me asking if he could come hang out with me in my bunker. He couldn't sleep and neither could I, so I decided to let him into my room, and let him in on what was transpiring.

While I was relaying everything to him, the feeling of intense paranoia and psychosis wandered back into my head. Noah was listening attentively as he does, but I couldn't look at him once again. I truly believed I was gonna see the being looking at me through Noah's beautiful eyes. I started having a difficult time speaking. My throat was tight, knees were weak, palms were sweaty.

"Hey Noah, could you open the door please? Please open the door," I directed.

He had shut it when he came into my room so we'd be courteous to our sleeping roommates, but he gladly opened it upon my request. When he sat back down, I exhaled a big sigh of relief. The possibility for a quicker escape made me feel immensely better. If I had to make a mad dash away from him, I no longer had a door closing me in with Noah/Nosferatu. I continued explaining, and confided in him what I was feeling.

"It's like the being is in my head, putting these thoughts in that I know aren't real but the paranoia becomes so intense out of nowhere that I become so overwhelmed. What if I get completely lost in the overwhelm and lose it?"

I was rambling at this point, "and Noah, I don't feel too far from losing it. This has never happened to me before, something affecting my mental state like this. I don't feel equipped to combat this. How does someone combat this? What are the *tools?*"

First, Noah offered one of those wide-eyed looks with an innocent smile that spoke for itself, like, "I don't know what to say or do but you're scaring me, haha." But Noah is so full of goodness, and while he may not have had specific answers to that very specific problem, understandably, his comforting and kind words reminded me that there's no way a being as snippy as little Nosferatu could thrive in the same space as Noah. Around 2am, Noah wandered back to his room in a sleepy stupor, and I flipped the lock on my door before stumbling into bed. I didn't fall asleep until the sun was rising.

That next day, I stayed holed up in the apartment. Experience the paranoia while surrounded by hoards of college students who are already likely possessed by their own demons? No thank you. No coffee shop on campus could bring enough comfort. Thinking back on that time, I realize how absolutely out of my right mind I would have seemed had one of my roommates come home during the day. Thankfully my roommates were busy with classes until the evening. Unfortunately, I was in the middle of the biggest smackdown yet between the being and my sanity.

Around 10am, you would have heard me yelling at little Nosferatu to get out of my bedroom and leave me alone. You would have heard me calling on my loved ones, spirit guides, and angels louder than necessary to protect me, my place, and all of my roommates. Around 11am, you would have smelled the sage I was aggressively wafting throughout the apartment, in every nook and cranny. Around noon, you would have found me pacing around my living room, grabbing my head and pleading for the being to scram.

"GET OUT OF MY HEAD! GET OUT OF MY ENERGY FIELD!" I would yell. I had the windows open, and at one point some people walked by and did a double take. All I could do was throw up the peace sign. Maybe they'd think I was just tripping on shrooms. I jumped when my phone started ringing, but I was happily surprised to see my momma's name on the screen. I picked up the phone and almost immediately, shamelessly started crying. The powerlessness I felt after one night of mental instability had me in shambles. In that moment I felt a heavy dread, like the being would never go away and, further, the feeling that it set off in me. I was stuck with it forever and ever and ever, for all of eternity, ever. And eternity is a long time. Part of me felt so relieved to be able to talk to my momma, because she didn't question my sanity one bit. But another part of me, the part that was being affected by the being, felt like I couldn't trust her either. I felt like the reality that I knew to be true was entirely fake, per the paranoia. I was in this void where only the being and me existed, and everything else was a facade. Including my momma on the phone. I was spiraling. There was so much crying. My picture was pasted in the dictionary next to the word "yikes".

"Momma, it's making me scared of everyone around me. It's making me think that my roommates are not real. It's making me think that I'm not actually on the phone with you right now, like this just isn't happening. I don't know what to do! I don't feel strong enough to deal with this. I don't know how to protect myself. How do you protect yourself from something like this? We don't even know what it is!"

"Oh boy Peanut, that's bad," my mom remarked.

For just a split second, I slipped out of the psychosis, only long enough to roll my eyes at my momma's dry response.

"But Morgan," she continued, "you need to knock it off. You are strong enough. You know you are. Stop allowing it to run you around. It's laughing now, Mo."

Heavy breathing

"Fill a bowl with saltwater and put it in your bedroom. That should help clean the energy," my momma offered. "Wait, it's saying, 'that won't work!' Do it, I think the entity is feeling threatened," I could hear in her voice that more advice was coming.

"Grandma is coming through to me right now. She's saying she's going to kick this thing's butt for you. She's with you, and she's saying that you don't have to be afraid because you are stronger than this. It's that simple. You are full of love and you're surrounded by love on this side and the other side. You're going to be okay, there's no question about that."

My heart was pounding out of my chest, and then out of my left ear.

"Morgan, Grandma is trying to communicate with you. Do you hear her? You might feel her on your left side. She's there with you."

I nodded, acknowledging her presence with me.

"Now that you know you're not alone, it's time to be strong. Grandma's saying that you need to pray. You need to ask your loved ones, spirit guides, and angels to assist you in this. That's what they're there for. They'll help you but only if you allow them. The entity is laughing again. Creepy," my momma concluded.

More heaving breathing

"Are you getting angry? I can feel that on you. Don't let it make you angry. That will feed its energy. You need to send it love. Imagine colorful hearts being sent from you to the entity. The other day when I encountered it in the kitchen I said to it, 'I'm going to give you a hug if you don't leave' and it ran off yelling, 'Noooooooo'. So when it comes around, tell it that you're only going to show it love. And really, truly send it love."

Momma the angel, teaching me to lead with love, even when battling multi-dimensional vampires.

"Are you gonna be okay, Pean?"

"Yeah..." I forced, even though I was still blubbering like a baby. With that, my momma hung up and I went to work. I confronted the entity, who I could now feel very strongly in the room with me. It went a little something like this:

"I am done feeling powerless around you. I am strong. I live in love. I only have love to give you at this point, so take it or leave it. Thank you for this experience. It has taught me what I need to know, and now I'm letting you go. I love you, but it's time for you to go."

I sat in the energy of love that I was conjuring up for a few moments, feeling empowerment from the light building within. I think it's important to highlight, especially in the thick of this section, that we all have the capacity to empower ourselves to a frequency at which we feel supported by connecting with love, or source energy. We can do this simply by creating a happy place in our minds, tapping into feelings of gratitude, love, and joy, and holding the feeling. I continued to empower myself in that moment by going to my happy place - sitting outside of the student union by Lake Mendota with my friends and a pitcher of Blue Moon, the sun shining down on us. I kept going back to that place every time it began to dissipate and I felt a twinge of paranoia. I'm not sure how long I was in that meditative ping-pong, but when I came out of that gentle stupor, I felt a peace that had escaped me for a few weeks. Such peace. I felt unstoppable. Unf***withable. Then my phone rang.

"Hi Mo, do you feel better?"

"Yeah Momma I do! I really do! I sent it love and sent it packing I think!" I was excitedly fist-pumping the air like they do on the Jersey Shore.

"Well I did cleanse your house with celestial light and I think I booted the thing out. He can't get back in, not for a bit anyways. It'll fade after a while but he's stuck outside for now. He can't reach you."

I like to think the result was a combination of both my momma and I's fabulous efforts.

From then on, the being came around less frequently. And when it did come around, the little Nosferatu was considerably weaker. I was once again able to look at my roommates without feeling paranoid, and I could even sleep with my lights off. Every so often when I was least expecting it, the paranoia would creep back in, but I felt empowered enough to defend myself. If I felt threatened beyond my capacity to handle it, I called my loved ones. They always came to the rescue. I conjured up that happy place in my mind's eye often, and that did wonders. The being lacked the power it once held. Or maybe I empowered myself to a frequency that was unreachable. How curious that choosing to focus on love rather than fear was the answer to my problem. So when they say love conquers all, maybe they're onto something.

    I have rewritten this experience multiple times, as everytime I leave it alone for a while and come back to it I see it with fresh eyes and a new perspective. I learn something new and important from it with every passing year that I put it down. That being said, I shared my truth from the experience of it at the time to lament the fact that I am always a student. I expand with every minute and catalyst. I learn as I go. This experience that I was privy to wasn't bad or good. It was just uncomfortable for me for obvious reasons. Yes, it was a low-vibrational experience that struck fear in me, but more than that it was a teacher; a catalyst. This was a lesson in the necessity and importance of self-empowerment that I had magnetized to me to learn from. Man, I learned. And boy did it inspire me to continue moving forward along my perfect spiritual journey. In hindsight, I realize that I was 100% fully empowered; I was being challenged to remember that empowerment. It also became clear to me that a spiritual awakening isn't always rainbows and butterflies, but I could make it a little easier by taking better, more intentional, care of myself.

    The first step in taking better care of myself was to move back home for a short time. Only for a short time. I was very against the idea, but I needed to reground myself in an environment that encouraged higher-vibrational behavior. So once again I was back at my momma's house half of the time, and the other half at my dad's house. I had picked up a job working at a golf course for the summer and fall, slinging drinks in the clubhouse, working the pro-shop, and doing kitchen prep for Friday night fish fry's. At the same time, I was continuing forward on my spiritual journey and working through the lessons that I brought upon myself at that time. That period of my life was about understanding energy. How it flowed, how I could take care of mine, how it affected others, and so forth.

    For a while I thought energy was a fickle witch, to put it eloquently. Unable to be tamed. At that point in my life I would have compared my relationship with energy to that of a teenager and a parent. Me, being the parent, and energy, being the rebellious and out of control kiddo. I couldn't get a handle on controlling my own energy, so protecting myself from outside energy was a whole other challenge. I know now that it is of the utmost importance to learn how to control your energy, which manifests in countless forms such as thoughts and emotions. Energy plays a monumental role in our everyday lives whether we recognize it or not. Everything is composed of energy. The physical objects around us, the people we walk this lifetime with, the feelings that burden or embolden us, the actions we take and the snowball effect that is set in motion as a result. As sentient human beings, capable of perception and feeling, it makes sense that we would do well to give attention to that which is the foundation for everything in existence. As an empath, that notion should be underlined, written in **bold**, and concluded by at least three exclamation marks. An empath is someone who has the ability to sense the energies of other beings. When we deny ourselves an awareness of energy, we often allow in unwarranted sensations and unwelcome attachments. Then we question why we feel so bad out of nowhere, why we're so exhausted, why we have little unwelcome shrimpy, snippy beings following us to coffee shops!

Let me be your prime example that energy must be cared for. For the longest time, I was undisciplined in taking care of myself physically, emotionally, and spiritually. I didn't attempt in the slightest to empower myself or protect myself from the energy that I was manifesting and attracting. As a result, I faced a lot of physical repercussions. And once things start manifesting in the physical, you *know* they've been brewing on an energetic level for a while. The entity was one repercussion that really brought this issue of needing to empower and protect myself to light. Another example were PK manifestations. And while I faced these repercussions myself, oftentimes so did the people around me. Sorry Momma.

After I moved back home, I really crashed for just a hot second. If you thought I had hit bottom before, not quite. My frequency was low, my emotions all willy-nilly. In the midst of working to take care of myself energetically, I realized that neglecting my energetic body went hand in hand with rejecting my emotions. Oh, yes, I had been one to repress and bottle up and keep my emotions hidden somewhere increasingly deep and dark, as we tend to do when we're hoping to bypass negative human emotions and experiences. But I only realized that this defense mechanism of repressing emotions was destructive to me and others once the lesson physically came to fruition for me to deal with. As I said, a lot has already been in the works energy-wise once things appear in the physical.

So what transpired is this. I bit my tongue on my emotions and repressed and held in and let all of the fear-based energy fester. Then I would energetically erupt like a volcano, the effects of which would reach those close by. My momma would show me scratches that showed up out of nowhere on her body, coincidentally at times that I locked myself down in my dark bedroom with only my angst and the songs of Imogen Heap to keep me company. It was as if my energetic frequency was sending a message to my momma to *STAY AWAY*. Psychokinesis is the ability to manipulate physical environments without physical interaction. It wasn't an ability that I wielded often, or with finesse. It was only ever accidental, brought to life by my inability to acknowledge my very human emotions. Psychokinesis can manifest in many unnerving forms, thus the term PK manifestations. Objects being moved to new locations or completely disappearing, scratches appearing on people, paintings on the wall swinging back and forth.

After brooding at work all day, I dove into my bed in the basement room at my momma's house. I had been sitting up for a few minutes flipping through channels when I noticed movement out of the corner of my eye. About three feet from me, a very large painting hung on the wall. And it was swinging back and forth. Not aggressive, off-the-hinges kind of swinging. But enough for me to question my sanity. I was stunned into immobility. As I continued staring, the painting continued swinging, not ceasing or slowing in the slightest. I watched the spectacle for two minutes, utterly baffled. When I realized that it wasn't stopping anytime soon, I jumped from under the covers and bolted up the stairs to my momma's room. I needed a witness.

"Momma! The painting on my wall is swinging!" I loudly whispered.

"What-"

"SWINGING!"

In her sleepiness, my momma followed me back downstairs, and to my excitement, the darn thing was still going.

I clapped my hands together excitedly, watching my momma's reaction.

"It's been swinging for a solid three minutes," I explained.

My momma chuckled, "did you bump it? Is your window open?" We examined all logical avenues of explanation, but to no avail.

"I was sitting in my bed for about ten minutes before I noticed it swinging. I didn't touch it. I hadn't even moved."

While we were trying to debunk the mysterious swinging painting, it kept on going with no shame. My momma reached out and stopped it, stilling the painting. It remained still. We gave it a little nudge to see how long it would swing on its own. And as would be expected, it didn't take long for the painting to come to a halt once more. There were maybe ten seconds of swinging at the most.

Beyond the swinging painting, which was pretty exciting from an objective point of view, I've experienced some other funky phenomena. Like the recliner chair I would sit in shaking vigorously. Waking up to small scratches across my chest and throat. No, I didn't scratch myself in my sleep. I was a notorious nail biter with nothing but nubs.

I compare that period of my spiritual awakening to those god-awful teenage years characterized by moodiness and brooding and angst, and being hungry *all of the time!* And just like teenagers have a tendency to do with life, I really convinced myself that I had the whole spiritual awakening thing figured out. But as my mom liked to remind me often while growing up when I acted like I knew it all, "my brain was not yet fully developed." I really had convinced myself for a while that the experiences I was slammed with on a daily basis would detail my life for the rest of time. I thought that's simply what being "spiritual" entailed. In reality, this phase was monumental in kicking off a higher energetic frequency. Like I mentioned earlier, my higher self knew what kind of lessons I needed to experience to get me where I needed to go. Very physical, concrete, undeniable, action-packed experiences that held no room for ignorance.

"Yeah, that ought to do the trick!" my higher self surmised, while physical me was rocking in the fetal position, attempting to integrate.

I could not go on in the same manner that I had been existing in and expect the process to get any easier. That was naive, and I refused to be naive! So I put on my big girl pants and went to work prioritizing all things spiritual.

♡ Chapter 7 ♡

Inspiring Beings w/ Fancy Names

Being back in Coleman allowed me a safe space to deal with my demons. The metaphorical and literal demons. And over the span of a few weeks, I came to understand something big. Per the Law of Attraction, I had been attracting both wanted and unwanted experiences. Yet, both the wanted and unwanted were exactly what my soul needed to expand. If only I had known this before the previous chapter of my life. Hindsight, am I right?

After spending some time back at home, on my best behavior, my frequency began to rise. And as my frequency rose, I attracted a more enjoyable path along my spiritual journey, characterized less by fear and increasingly more and more by love. This state of love ushered in a multitude of frequency resonating catalysts for me to experience and learn from. Catalysts that taught lessons through joy rather than pain or fear. I had done a complete 180, in the best way. Meditation became the most important part of my day. I drank green tea instead of coffee, and more water than my body could keep up with. I delved into crystals and tarot cards and pendulums and other modalities of healing and strengthening intuition and connection. And the more I researched and experienced, the more I understood the power of love as a foundation for my beingness. Slowly but surely my experiences were primarily about excitement and elation, gratitude and inspiration.

* * * * *

I have often been teased with quick glimpses and sudden, out-of-nowhere experiences. It's a fun product of the circumstances. Early on a Sunday afternoon I was dozing off into an accidental nap as I frequently did, when I gained consciousness to the feeling of my body sinking. Where was I going? Naturally, my astral body was venturing out of my physical body to take a spin on the astral plane. This usually happened when I least expected it. If I planned to astral travel, I was normally left disappointed. But if I hoped to score a few hours of peaceful snoozing, forget about it – I'd be faced with bizarre astral plane happenings whether I liked it or not. So that particular time when I felt a part of myself separating from my physical, human shell, I said what the heck and let it happen.

I popped my astral hands out from my physical body, followed by my arms, my head, and finally my upper body. I was half committed to the astral plane, half stuck in this physical "reality" still. But I couldn't see. That seemed to be a common theme for me when taking those astral trips. It either took a while for my vision to develop, or it simply didn't kick in as a working sense. During that particular trip, my vision was initially black.

As I was adjusting to the astral plane, I felt a new energy overcome me. Normally I felt unnerved when entering the astral plane. I was never sure what kind of experience I'd be privy to and in the past I associated astral traveling with uncomfortable experiences. Yet at that moment, the energy that overcame me was unlike any I had experienced so far in my travels. I was actively contemplating the fear that made up the very foundation of my past astral travel experiences when a light began to manifest. It grew from a small dot of bright contrast in the dark void until the light became distinguishable as aqua blue. It always excites me when my vision works while my physical eyes are closed. That tells me that my third-eye is up and running, ready for business.

This bright aqua light blossomed, becoming brighter and growing larger to take up more of my vision. It was ethereal; the energy made me feel miniscule and grand all at once. It comforted me in a setting that I had typically found a lack of comfort in. It made me excited, not nervous as the astral plane tended to do.

"She sees bright colors in her head, woah."

I know, it *sounds* lame in limited words, but the beauty is in the eye of the beholder and I felt way too many sensations in that short experience to not be moved by the aqua energy that was presenting itself to me. It was more than the appearance of a light. It felt glorious, like unconditional love curled up in a soft blanket with warm chocolate chip cookies and sunlight and a puppy! All the best feelings, and then some, rolled into one, transpiring before me while I existed in a state of perfect awareness.

And as the energy enveloped the entirety of my vision, the shape of a being appeared within the aqua. First only faintly, but slowly with more vividness and detail. The face and features outlined by contrasting hues of blue. The hair, considerably lighter than the face, floating like slow waves. Eyes that twinkled like stars from another galaxy; stars that my humanness had not experienced in the Milky Way. The being appeared female, with delicate, humanesque features. I knew innately she wasn't human, but appearing in the likeness to connect with me. Something about her was too otherworldly. Perhaps it was the fact that she was blue and flawless! Her eyes regarded me intensely, but not uncomfortably. And as clearly as if someone were speaking directly into my ear, she called to me.

"Morgan."

The feminine being called my name four times, each time a bit louder. Her voice was smooth and pure, like she was created to guide a meditation. She was patient, simply trying to connect with me when I was ready. But honestly the whole thing overwhelmed me in the moment and my fight or flight instincts kicked in. I mentally began to shake myself, which is my tactic for escaping the astral plane and waking my physical body back up. Slowly I regained control of my dormancy, and shot up in my bed. Everything was exactly as I had left it. Except my ears felt like water had just been running through each of their canals. I reached my hand up to my ears to see if anything was out of the norm. Nothing. And then I mentally face-palmed myself.

"Stupid! Stupid! Stupid! Morgan, c'monnnnnnnn."

I flopped on my back dramatically. Why would I shake myself awake from that experience? What if I was about to communicate with a being that had answers to my long-list of questions? What if I was about to be let in on some secrets to this "reality" or the real realities *beyond*? I took a second to appreciate what had just occurred, and then I resorted to begging.

"I was very, very dumb. That was so human of me. Please come back, I'll be better. Now that I know this is coming I'll be receptive and less overwhelmed and more open to communicating and *better*. Come back! Here, let's try this again."

I pulled the covers back up to my chin and slowed my breathing, ready to jump back into the moment. But it wasn't in the cards this time around. I blew it. The chance came and went.

I pondered on the woman for the next couple of days. And in the middle of one of those days, deep in meditation, I was given the answer that the being was my higher self. My highest and purest self in a recognizable form. That meditation was my indoctrination to a deeper connection with the version of myself that knew all. See you next time I'm meant to see you, Morgan. Or whatever name the highest and purest version of myself resonates with. Maybe Scarlet?

Traversing through my mind and soul in meditation daily brought memories back to the surface. Some memories that I didn't realize I had, and others that I had buried away for a rainy day. Well, it was a rainy summer day, the kind where the sun still shines, and I came across a memory that proved to be quite interesting. Back in my freshman dorm room, Shitty Witte if you recall, I spent a lot of time napping, yes. But I also meditated often. And one random day I was in that tiny dorm room, falling further into meditation when I so vividly heard, "I am Ra."

I gave this greeting the minimal contemplation and research at the time, per a lack of interest in *anything*. So flashforward to the meditation on this rainy summer day, where the same words greeted me loud and clear. Slowly spoken, enunciated, and in a deep tone. I pulled my headphones from my ears and took the stairs two at a time to my laptop upstairs, ready to do what I did best - research.

And what I was led to was a collective consciousness of advanced souls that went by the short, sweet, and easy to remember name, Ra. This collective consciousness first became known in our current "reality" here on Earth back in the 80's, when a research team member acted as a conduit for channeling through to the much higher frequency of Ra. The research team, guided by Ra, was able to bring through to our current "reality" something truly astounding; deep knowledge that is becoming more understood with every day that passes. The major takeaway that I have gathered from researching the conversations with Ra is the Law of One. In my humblest interpretation of the Law of One, knowing that I am a fickle human whose memory of the divine is still in a stage of restoration, is that all is simply one. We human beings are all individualized aspects of the same source. All that is, is part of that source. Every thought, miniscule or colossal, in physical form or a less dense form, is connected to the infinite, the one. I read through the collection of conversations that were had between Ra and the research team, spending days contemplating certain ideas that went right over my head. It's not light reading, but it is a read comprised of the purest light. I encourage you to pursue your own understanding of the Law of One, through your own research and particular form of contemplation.

So when I experienced that second meditation hearing "I am Ra" so clearly, I knew I was on my soul's path, moving and shaking and getting things done with the ideas of love and connection leading the way. I've said it before and I'll say it again. How lucky am I to share this current lifetime of mine connecting with beings that encourage unconditional love and endless support? My connection with Ra was brief, but monumental. I started remembering that I'm actually the Morgan who likes to smile at people, who encourages connection and understanding, rather than the Morgan who wore hoodies and headphones, closing out and pushing away. I started remembering what living in a state of love felt like, as opposed to a state of constant fear.

Furthermore, the small connection I had to Ra opened me up to more connections with spiritual teachers who unknowingly, or maybe knowingly, were huge catalysts in increasing the momentum of my personal, conscious spiritual expansion. Another that I happened upon by the reference of a like-minded friend who also questioned reality was Drunvalo Melchizedek, a spiritual researcher and much higher dimensional being in human form. In my humblest interpretation again, Drunvalo Melchizedek is most notable for defining the merkaba, which is the light body that surrounds each of our physical bodies. This light body, when understood and activated to its fullest potential, gives us the intrinsic ability to travel multidimensionally. Drunvalo Melchizedek also speaks on topics such as the lost civilization of Atlantis, pyramids, the power and memory that crystals hold, sacred geometry, and so forth, all explored through a state of unconditional love that transcends this dense, current "reality". I know, it's a lot. Explore what resonates with you at this moment, and allow the other things to come back when and if they resonate. There are no expectations and there is no pressure on what your personal spiritual journey should entail. There is, however, a surplus of fascinating and otherworldly topics to research, so stay curious!

With the vague description that I gave of a merkaba in the forefront of your mind, I had a meditation that seemed to connect with the esoteric idea. I was simply lounging on the couch midday in the living room at my momma's house. The sun was shining in, my momma was watching Ancient Aliens. I was cozied deep under a blanket, so lounging quickly turned into astral traveling as it so often does in my experience. One second I was laying on the couch, my kitty-cat Georgie boy cuddled by my head, and the next I was laying in the grass in our front yard. I was immediately aware of my circumstances, and aptly floated up into the air just because I could. I flitted around the yard for a few moments, rising to gain a higher vantage point to survey the land. And then a thought popped into my head to go visit my dad's house. Not a snap of the fingers later and I was there, floating up by the ceiling in our tall living room. The house was filled with sunshine. I remember seeing particles of dust floating around in the beams of light entering through the many windows. It was peaceful and warm and quiet and empty, until I saw myself no older than the age of 11 bound down the stairs into the kitchen. There I was, floating near the ceiling, watching as a younger version of myself danced around the kitchen, unaware of the time warp that was occurring. I watched on with curious contemplation, unsure of why I ended up at this place in time and space. Unsure of *how* I ended up there. Happy. She looks happy, I thought to myself. And so I stayed away, watching from my vantage point on a different plane entirely. A thought popped into my head, noticing her childlike innocence, her shameless inner child still reverberating through all dimensions. That experience made me realize that that singular moment of dancing through the kitchen as a young girl was still occurring, although hard for me to wrap my brain around. My inner child is still dancing shamelessly, and it was time that I awakened that knowledge and applied it to the current now. No more repressing that shiznit.

  But that's not even the point of this astral travel/meditation experience. That was just a little gift to me, from me. All too soon, my astral travel took a curious turn. I was no longer floating in my house, but rather was simply existing in a pitch black void. There was no fear. And I had no body. I was a conscious part of the whole that I was surrounded by. And my purpose of being in that state at the time was to construct my merkaba. This was clear to me. I didn't question it, as it felt right.

  The merkaba is an energetic star tetrahedron, whose two tetrahedrons spin super fast opposite each other when activated. This divine vehicle, whose name literally translates to light-spirit-body, allows us the ability to connect with source energy. And once we fully realize our connection to source energy, we can create anything and everything. I know this idea is a lot to take in, but the point was that I felt, while in this meditative dream state, that I was consciously aware of and being called to engineer my merkaba. So I said out loud in the void to no one and to everything all at once, "I'm going to create my merkaba now". These words were a declaration, and the Universe respects the hell out of clear declarations. It was as if a starting pistol went off at a track; the energy was off and racing. In the black void, I saw these beautiful cerulean lights materialize, growing and racing around my body, looking more and more purposeful. I was spinning and the light was spinning, and you would think I would be overwhelmed in that vortex of energy but I knew deep within that this was a good experience; a big moment. Intuitively, I molded these lights around my body into a sphere. The light continued to expand and manifest, taking on a pattern that looked familiar. Soon, the flower of life surrounded me. The flower of life is important in sacred geometry, bringing light to the fact that we are all connected. Look it up, and I'm sure you'll recognize it.

The cerulean lights morphed again, dancing around my beingness into the perfect structure. Once I understood that the process of whatever I had just experienced was complete, I started flying, though different from flying in my astral travels. I was limitless in time and space and dimensions. I can't explain the feeling of infinite energy. I know I only touched on a small piece of what infinite energy has to offer, but it was colossal relative to what I knew prior. It couldn't have lasted more than a few seconds, but the feeling I experienced has stuck with me all this time. I'd like to tap into it again when divine timing gives me the go ahead.

As I often do when I'm taken aback by what I experience in my astral travels, dreams, or meditations, I got too excited and woke up to my very heavy, very dense physical body. I bolted upright, startling George who was still curled up by my head. I startled my momma too, who was sitting only three feet away from me. Only three feet away from some kind of incomprehensible time warp / interdimensional vacation.

"Momma you will not believe what just happened!" I blurted out, followed by a fast rambling of everything that I could still remember from what just transpired.

"I felt like you went away for a bit. You had so much energy pooling over your body," my momma explained.

It's incredible and mind-boggling and so curious what experiences there are to be experienced. That was another story to add to the notes in my phone; a story that renewed any feelings of disenchantment towards my spiritual expansion. Suffice to say, elation is a powerful human feeling. But I'm guessing that incredible feeling of elation will be no match for what will be remembered of source and my true beingness on my spiritual expansion to come.

Drunvalo's teachings came at the exact right moment in my life, as divine timing would have it no other way. His books were quick reads for me, though the content took awhile to absorb fully. I was just so excited and mystified, and was trying to take in as much as I could in a short time. You know when you just can't put a good book down? Some of what he spoke of still hasn't sunk in or been understood by my puny, puny brain, like sacred geometry. I may be a fickle human most days, but I am nothing if not consistent in my aversion to anything mathematics. But the main takeaway that I had from his teachings, the idea that I have worked to incorporate into my life and give energy to more and more everyday is that of unconditional love. His work helped me to remember the understanding that was already deep within me, and within all of us, that all beings are connected, and derived from the same source. Our current "reality" characterized by variation of every kind is really just a result of the very creative right-brain of source. What a wondrous and beautiful and painful and humbling piece of art you have rendered, Universe. And to think that each and every one of us is a muse for the creation of that piece. Keep that in mind when your ego makes you think that you're anything less than an unconditionally adored divine being.

When I say "reality" with quotation marks, it's an idea that resonates deeply within me inspired by Drunvalo Melchizedek and many others. This idea is that what we perceive as reality is actually just an illusion, a classroom, a simulation if you will. Which I will. I have always thought this was a simulation, but I guess it used to hold more of a grim connotation in my mind. At one point I convinced myself that we were all existing within a game like *The Sims*, controlled by a kid behind a computer. Except in this version we advanced enough to experience consciousness. I really disliked that fearful perspective. In *reality*, we are energetic beings experiencing life on Earth only for a short time to accumulate soul-level experiences for expansion. This physical existence is a beautiful and tragic illusion that we brave, and somewhere deep down we remember that. But don't just take my regurgitated perspective of his words. I encourage you to read Drunvalo Melchizedek's inspiring and enlightening books so that you may come to conclusions that resonate deeply and personally with you.

On top of those supportive spiritual catalysts that aided in my spiritual expansion, I also happened upon Abraham Hicks. Abraham is a collective group consciousness that has transcended our physical reality, existing in a much lighter dimension than ours. The group consciousness's messages are relayed through Esther

Hicks, for the purpose of spreading the powerful understanding of the Law of Attraction. One of my favorite topics to research and discuss and share! Abraham Hicks explains that feelings associated with uninhibited joy and elation are the energy of source, that which we all derive from; that which creates all that is. To tap into this source energy is to have the ability to bring what you desire into your "vortex" and manifest! Vortex, meaning alignment to that source energy. Once you're in the metaphorical and literal energetic vortex, nothing can inhibit you aside from that pesky human ego that we all cling to so hard. Once again, I encourage you to research the plentiful videos and books and workshops that Abraham and Esther Hicks have to offer. It's important that these deeper understandings resonate with you personally, and that conclusions are based on your own experiences rather than mine.

    It turns out that I had been living the lifestyle that Abraham Hicks supports for a long time, aside from the every once in a while emotional low that I'd experience as a fickle and expanding human. I was most definitely *not* in the vortex last chapter. But when aligned with source unknowingly, a powerful understanding of the best outcome already belonging to me was always part of my outlook. Call it what you will. Optimism. A glass-half full approach. Being too damn cheerful and always looking on the brightside. All I knew is that I *knew* things and stuff would work out in the way they were supposed to. I remember I would argue with my dad when I was younger, defending this very topic before I understood it. I'm sure to him I sounded so naive.

    "I'm never going to go into a career that makes me unhappy or unfulfilled," I would state unrelentingly, arms crossed and everything.

    My dad would scoff, "You need to be able to support yourself, Mo! You'll need to have a job in a field that offers security, and sometimes you're not gonna enjoy the work but that's life."

    "Nope. I refuse."

    And for the most part I've stuck to that philosophy, always gravitating towards opportunities that resonated at the time. Leaving when the experience was no longer offering me fulfillment. And when I'm in the mood for a particular experience to be satiated, I bring the idea into my vortex and allow it to cross my path. I'm determined to demonstrate it on a grand scale someday soon to prove to my dad, amongst many others, that we have the awesome power to create our realities; that living in a state of love opens so many doors that fear could never.

All of that being said, I am so grateful for these spiritual teachers that have encouraged my pursuit into different areas of spirituality; into different areas of myself that I didn't know existed or made sense. I will always consider myself a student while in this physical reality, and even beyond. But that point in time with those teachers and catalysts was the turning point towards real, diligent, and slightly-more-disciplined appreciation for the curriculum. Give me all the gold stars!

* * * * *

The esoteric experiences continued, as did my spiritual expansion. Meditation was likened to a form of studying. And like I said, I was out for all the gold stars. Meditation became a daily habit again, and sometimes multiple times a day. Oftentimes, when I meditated, I was lulled so deeply into my own head, or maybe out of my head. It would feel as though I were somewhere entirely different than this physical plane. Just on the precipice of conscious awareness, but just out of reach of my physical body. My meditations had changed dramatically at this point in time compared to chapters prior. Now I followed no routine, only listening to my body for what would lead to mindfulness in each moment. Sometimes that meant envisioning the train, other times that meant laying in quiet contemplation of whatever passed through the forefront of my mind. Music or no music. Beats on low in the background or drowning out every idea in my head. It was twenty minutes before supper time one night when I decided to treat myself to a short meditation, stationed in my basement bedroom at my momma's house. I pulled a light blanket over me and started up some binaural beats. 432 hz, baby, which is the natural frequency that the Universe resonates at. Give me all of the healing! I was in deep, and soon lost track of myself as though I was sleeping. And then I found myself again, but I was no longer lying in my bed with the blanket and headphones. Instead, I was sitting on the floor in the back-storage area of our basement. Criss-cross on the cement, chilling with the spiders and the dust and all of the antique dish sets my momma collected from garage sales. Completely lucid and slightly confused.

"Erm. Why am I here?" I questioned out loud, wondering if I just teleported for the first time. But no, I could understand then that I hadn't teleported because upon further inspection, I felt funny. A funniness that characterizes a lack of physicality. I was dreaming. Lucid dreaming, to be specific. Lucid dreamers are aware of their dream state, although that awareness can vary. One experience may entail full awareness, and the ability to control every aspect of the dream in strong detail. Another experience may have the dreamer teetering back and forth between awareness and confusion, unable to commit. Isn't that incredible? We have the ability to enter a space where manifestation is immediate if we can tap into that awareness. It makes you wonder how effortless it could be to manifest so quickly in this current awareness we call "reality", if only we understood our power. Curiouser and curiouser. Still within these dreams of full awareness, things can occur seemingly independent of your own conscious creation. Back to my dream!

While I was sitting on the floor, contemplating why I dreamt myself into the storage area of our basement, I noticed a mirror ahead of me. And of course human nature led me to look into the reflection. And *of course* there was a freaky, old-timey, little boy standing behind me also looking into the mirror, twiddling his thumbs. My aversion to old-timey children reinforced.

I threw my hands over my eyes and chanted a mantra to soothe myself.

"Don't look at him. Don't look at him. Don't look at him. He'll go away."

When I snuck a peek between my fingers, the boy was nowhere to be found. It's not you, child, it's me. I have scary movie-induced trauma about kids like you that needs to be healed. It was then that I heard my step-dad talking from the kitchen directly up above me.

"It's getting bad outside really quick. A big storm is coming."

Was Todd making a cameo appearance in my dream?

Cue another unexpected visitor. A very large man, who I have never laid eyes on before, was heading my way. Unlike the small child in drab clothes, I knew I wouldn't be able to just cover my eyes this time and make the man disappear. So I watched in equal curiosity and trepidation as he made his way toward me. I watched as he passed me. And I watched as he headed in the direction of the stairs that led up from the basement into our kitchen. Before ascending, we made eye contact, but only briefly. He smiled, too. That was brief as well. And that was after I sent out a brief request for protection from my loved ones. The guy looked like he could pick me up with one hand and hail-mary me like Rodgers for a touchdown.

The man didn't stop to chat. That was fine by me. I was perturbed to see this large man so vividly strolling through my house; my lucid dream. This man was probably 6'4, with a large belly held up in denim overalls. He was a farmer. Aside from the overalls providing me context clues, it was just something that I knew about him. He scared me because I didn't expect him, but I wasn't afraid of his intentions. He had that big and bad… teddy bear look. And energy doesn't lie. His energy was chill. Nonthreatening.

So the man reached the stairs, and slowly made his way up. While I was taking him in, I could hear my momma and Todd talking from the kitchen. Were they actually playing very minor roles in my lucid dream or was I half awake, hearing their conversations as they made supper? Either way, as I tend to do, I yelled out for my momma.

"What?" My momma yelled back to me.

"COME DOWNSTAIRS RIGHT NOW!" I commanded.

As the man made his way up the stairs, my momma made her way down. I watched as they passed each other, neither acknowledging the other. It was a very bizarre experience to be privy to. When I'm just living my life, I never see spirits that vividly as though they were just another person in the here and now. But in this lucid dream, which felt like real life, I watched my momma and this man cross paths and continue on as though nothing happened. I wonder how often that happens to any one of us as we carry on completely unaware, believing that this "reality" is the extent of existence.

But within this lucid dream I was shocked that my momma hadn't been phased by the man passing her. He was so clear. Very physical. Much real. After the man disappeared upstairs and my momma had fully descended into the basement, I questioned her.

"Did you see the man walk past you??"

"I felt someone, but I couldn't see them," she explained.

When she spoke, she didn't speak to me. She was facing away from me. I was experiencing *another* facet of this bizarre lucid dream.

"Can you see me?" I questioned my momma slowly, just a tad bit on edge because, even though I knew I was dreaming, I felt so alive and real and connected with the environment I was in. Part of me was scared that I would be stuck somehow in that dream state forever, with no one able to sense me. My childhood fear of eternity stumbled back in for a second. All of this really just goes on and on and on, huh?

"Barely," she replied in a confused manner, examining the area where my voice was coming from.

And then an energetic shift occurred.

"Why do I feel funny?" I questioned out loud. I felt less physical than before, if that makes sense. As though I wasn't completely there. And I likely was *not* completely there. I was half hanging on to the lucid dream, and half ready to eat the din-din being whipped up by my momma and stepdad in waking "reality".

"You can still hear me, right?" I questioned my momma.

"I can barely hear you now. What's going on Morgan?!"

My momma was frantic. So was I. Get me out of here before I cease to exist to everyone around me!

I reached a hand out to my momma and laced our fingers together. She looked at her hand, knowing that I was holding it but confused at the disconnect between us. With every second, I felt my energy shifting, becoming nothing or perhaps expanding into everything.

"I'm disappearing! Help me get out of here!" I yelled as loud as I could so my momma would hear me.

And suddenly I was being pulled by my momma at lightning speed. We were speeding by. Limitless. Bound to no one place or space in time. Everything was moving in fast-forward. The world around me turned into a time-travel, characterized by bright streaks of color. This experience was brief, but impactful. Writing this now I can still vividly recall what I saw, how I felt. Though comforted by my momma's tight grasp on my hand, I called out to my spirit guides, angels, and loved ones for empowerment and guidance as we transcended that dreamstate. Please help me get back to my bed before supper! It's taco night!

And just like that, I was back in my bed. Out of the vortex of fast colors and unease. The binaural beats, still playing through my headphones and the quilt, pulled up to my chin. I opened my eyes and, shockingly but not surprisingly, the large man from my lucid dream was standing at the foot of my bed. But gone just as quickly as he came.

Now envision me bolting up the stairs two at a time. When I made it to the kitchen, I blurted out the whole experience to my momma and Todd, excited about what transpired. But even more excited that they could both hear and see me finally. It turns out that Todd's comment about the storm that I heard in my lucid dream was actually him in real life. But the momma in my dream was not real life Momma. At least.. it wasn't her consciously, knowingly bringing me back to this "reality" for taco night. Perhaps she was preparing the toppings and entered into a meditative state, whereupon part of her soul decided to pop in on my lucid dream. I wouldn't put it past her for being nosy. The whole thing was all very *Coraline* in retrospect. Albeit, less evil. And no button eyes.

It also turns out that the man I described from my lucid dream very accurately matched a man that my momma had connected with only a few days prior in a reading. The man she connected with had passed away while working on his farm. So why did he show up in my dream? Perhaps he wanted to key us into the fact that he was still around. Did he have another message he wanted to get across to his loved ones? Did he have unfinished business? Was he just passing through to say hello before moving on? After that dream, I never felt him around or experienced any kind of visitation from him again. My momma hasn't either. To be continued, I suppose!

Those daily meditations offered some unexpected experiences, to say the least. Some days I simply achieved a half hour of mindful contemplation, and others it seemed I journeyed through time and space. Another time I was meditating when I found a lighter part of my being disengaging. One minute I was aware of my physical body lying in my bed with binaural beats pulsing in my ears, and the next I was entering the living room of my Grandma Russell's house in the next town over. How peculiar that I would automatically choose this destination for my astral travels, I thought to myself. The lights were off in the house, and the sun didn't shine in like it should have in the mid-afternoon. But I wasn't curious enough about these details to ponder longer. I simply floated over to the light switch and illuminated the living room. To my surprise, the entire room was filled with balloons! Balloons everywhere! Clusters tied together and single, lonesome balloons. Balloons on the ceiling and balloons covering the floor. One of every color imaginable, and then some. A pretty spectacular "hello" from my Grandpa Russell, whose love languages were balloons and pennies.

"Love you, Grandpa. Thank you for this," I spoke to the balloon-filled room, knowing that my grandpa was listening from somewhere beyond that plane.

And soon enough, I opened my eyes to find myself back in my physical body, smiling like a kid in a toy store who just got the coolest gift. Man, my loved ones are always outdoing themselves.

Here's another example to prove that.

It was just another random day, as it often tends to be. Just another random day where I felt low and doubtful and all those other feelings that spring up from time to time, per the result of being an energetic being encapsulated in a dense physical body. Contentedness? I don't know her. Excitement for everyday life? I wasn't at the moment. Motivation? Where are you? I had a laundry list of errands to run and things to be done, but not a whole lot of energy to get me moving and shaking. But, as we have to do sometimes, I forced myself to act on my stupor and made my way out the door. Into my car I plopped with the least bit of enthusiasm. I put the key in the ignition, started the engine, and watched the time pop up.

4:44pm.

That's my grandma's number. Earlier I mentioned how repeating numbers have significance, and this is one number that holds very personal significance to my momma and me. I'm not sure when we began connecting the number to my beautiful grandma's spirit, but that's just the way it was from some random moment onward.

I smiled to myself and didn't think much further into it other than it being a happy coincidence. But may I remind you that there is no such thing as a coincidence. It's just a word the government made up. I turned the volume on the radio up, first and foremost, but no music was coming through. That was bizarre. It hadn't happened before. So, I sat for a moment with the volume on high to see if the radio station would kick in, but it didn't. Instead, in a very soft feminine tone and slow manner, came the single word, "Hi".

Just a simple "hi" with no conversation preceding or following. Did I really just hear that? Was that my sweet and gentle Grandma Halfmann popping in to literally say hello? I sat in the driver's seat in awe, but only for a moment when the radio made a staticky noise and began blasting music through my speakers at full volume in the middle of a song. I think it was Maroon 5. With renewed vigor, I sped to town to tackle the day. If my grandma could do the most to remind me that she's near, then I could put a little pep in my step and embrace that awesome gift to the fullest, even on the hard, human days.

Around the time that I acclimated back to living at home, my momma and I took a trip to Madison to pick up the rest of my furniture before my lease officially ended. We decided to make a momma/daughter weekend out of it, with a hotel and everything. My affinity for hotels is only rivaled by the continental breakfast that those very hotels serve. Naturally that weekend we found ourselves at the spiritual shop on State Street that we perused a time or two before. We each signed up for readings, and were pleasantly surprised to see that the same psychic-medium who read for us once before was in that day. Jean-Anne, who we came to establish a connection with, recognized us from the past as we walked into her space. We hugged like old friends, caught up, and dove into the tarot-type readings she conducted. Just like our first readings with her, aside from the whole ghost-boyfriend debacle that stumped everyone, it was accuracy all around. I laughed. My momma cried. We had a wonderful time. At the beginning of my reading, while shuffling with my not-so-nimble hands to fill the deck with my energy, a card aggressively flew out. While I would have assumed it to be a random card that needed to be placed back in with the others, Jean-Anne explained that it fell out for a reason. We would come back to it at the end of the reading. Well, it was the end so, with a pause for effect and a little dramatic flair, Jean-Anne flipped the card over and gasped.

"What?!" I braced.

She looked up at me excitedly, "This is the best card in the deck! See how it has no number on it, unlike the others? It is the card for making things happen. You can make a wish and it will come true," she nodded at me encouragingly.

So Jean-Anne placed the card in my hand, and I gave my cheesy, yet heart-felt, wish to the Universe. I can't wait until it comes to fruition. In the meantime, I'll keep believing in spiritual teachers like Ra, Drunvalo Melchizedek, Abraham-Hicks, my momma, and Jean-Anne. I'll keep believing in the divine timing and flow of the Universe. And I'll keep believing in that wish I made on the tarot card, because it's a good one.

♡ Chapter 8 ♡

I Wanna Be Sassy & British

In my quest to understand further, and further develop my connection with the spirit world, my momma and I had the great opportunity of doing a workshop with Mavis Pittilla. A world-renowned psychic medium, Mavis Pittilla helped me see a new perspective on all of this craziness. Before her two-day workshop exploring psychic and mediumship abilities, I felt separate from the spirit world. I wanted spirit to prove itself to me, when in reality I needed to do a whole lot of proving to the spirit world. It's that damn human ego that I keep talking about. It needs to go!

The workshop spanned two days, both days from 9am to 4pm. By the end of each day I was exhausted, immediately falling asleep in the passenger seat of my momma's car on our drive home. My momma heard of the workshop months prior and signed us both up. It was my first time at this kind of thing, but my momma had been around the block once or twice before. She has attended workshops put on by James Van Praagh twice, and grew exponentially from the experience. It was time to take me along. Time to let me fly. I knew the basics, and now I needed to put that miniscule knowledge into action.

On the first day, we were invited into a light studio, enticed with free coffee or tea and the opportunity to receive a lesson from Mavis Pittilla, psychic/medium extraordinaire. The room filled up a few minutes before day one of the workshop began. There were about thirty participants in total. I was the youngest by far, but I bet I looked more excited than anyone else. I couldn't sit still in my chair. I was buzzing from the excitement, nerves, or coffee, but really it didn't matter because I was *doing the thing*.

Then the great, great Mavis Pittilla flung the double doors open, allowing the most beautiful, bright light and energy to precede her before walking in to greet us. She floated down the short aisle past us to the front of the room. Grace, her middle name. Angels were singing. Goosebumps were rising. I had died and went to Heaven. And thank God Mavis Pittilla was in the building. I knew she'd do justice communicating to my mom that I was blissed out beyond this physical plane.

This was monumental for me. I fumbled for my notebook and pen, ready to write down every word that Mavis Pittilla uttered.

"Hello!" she began, making even that simple word seem incredibly humble.

H-e-l-l-o, I wrote.

Mavis spent the beginning of the workshop introducing herself and her partner, Jean Else. She shared her story, in her wonderful British accent, which I will not reiterate considering she has one of the best books I've ever read detailing her journey. *Droplets of God.* Do yourself a favor and read it. Once the initial shock of her presence was diminishing, we got to work. We were to fill out brief surveys of our abilities, and explain what we hoped to achieve from the workshop.

Level of experience? The piece of paper asked.

Beginner, and very excited to be here. Thanks for having me.

What do you hope to get out of this experience?

I don't even remember what I put, to be honest, but I got above and beyond what I expected out of the workshop at the end of the two days.

Day one was dedicated to our psychic abilities. We would be studying techniques, expanding on our awareness, and putting what we had learned into action. Early in the day, Mavis Pittilla led us in guided meditation. We the students sat upright and determined, receptive and calm in our chairs as the scene was verbally laid out for us.

"Alright, now I want you to imagine you are walking down a path. What does your path look like?" Mavis Pittilla questioned.

With my mind's eye, the scene was unfolding before me. A field in the mountains around me, with a pleasant dirt path below my bare feet.

Mavis Pittilla continued, "Ahead of you, a bridge unfolds on your path. What does the bridge look like?"

A rickety, but charming, wooden bridge with rails up to my chest. I crossed the bridge, enveloped by a bright sun shining down on me.

"And after you cross the bridge, you run into an obstacle in the middle of your path. What is this obstacle? How do you get past it?"

A wolf stood before me. Both of us sentient beings at a standstill. A staring contest ensued for a moment, until I realized my place. To me, the wolf was a physical manifestation of many things. Fear. Power. Wisdom. Fear was my initial reaction. Quickly, I acknowledged the fear. Power radiated from the wolf. I acknowledged its power. And finally wisdom. The wolf was beyond me in regard to wisdom, and therefore I thought it wise to surrender. The way to circumvent the obstacle came to me without deep contemplation. To honor and surrender to the fear, power, and wisdom, I simply knelt before the wolf and bowed my head. I acknowledge my fears. I honor the power within me and outside of myself. I surrender to that which I don't understand thus far. I surrendered to the Universe, in wolf-form. In my mind's eye, when I looked up from my bowed position, the wolf was no longer before me. I suppose I passed the test.

"And you continue past the obstacle, having taken the necessary steps to get around it. At this point, you reach a mountain. What is the mountain made of?"

Red, dry rock. A little crumbly, but sturdy under my bare feet. Little did I know that this was foreshadowing. That silly Universe knows how to construct a story alright, with little breadcrumb clues here and there.

"You begin your ascent up the mountain. Half way on your climb, you come across a goblet containing a liquid. What do you do with the goblet and the liquid?"

Well, it didn't feel like I had a right to drink the mysterious liquid in the mysterious goblet. Plus, I was taught to never take unsolicited drinks. So I raised the goblet to my nose and inhaled the essence, as though I were inhaling pure and light energy and exhaling heavy and stagnant energy. I set the goblet back down onto the red rocks and continued onward.

"You finally reach the top of the mountain. What a journey you have been on. You have grown in many ways and been renewed. How do you intend on getting down from the mountain now?" Mavis Pittilla challenged.

Without thinking too deeply, I envisioned myself not getting down from the top but instead floating higher. Five feet, then ten feet, then twenty feet, until I held a perspective of the world around me. I felt I could see the entire journey I had traveled, both in a physical/material sense, as well as a spiritual way. I saw the dirt path and the bridge, the wolf ambling by and the mountain top. I saw my fears diminish, and experienced my soul stepping into my power. The strength that I had deep within me.

And simply because it felt right at that position of mine high up in the sky, I began to shine a white light that encircled me and filled me. It expanded until the entire vision in my mind's eye was healing, white light.

Shortly after, Mavis Pittilla brought us back. Us students slowly began to stretch, popping our eyes open, leaving the beautiful places that we experienced so effortlessly. Mavis Pittilla asked for volunteers to share their experiences with each of the steps we came across in our meditations. As you'd expect, our experiences were all over the spectrum, varying greatly. Some walked dirt paths, others concrete sidewalks, and then there was my momma who walked down a glowing and smooth marble walkway. Our bridges were characterized by wooden planks, shakey ropes, moss and stone, or, like my momma, marble ingrained with crystals. Some people were presented with animals like me, brick walls, storms, and toxic versions of themselves as the obstacle. As other students had shared their experiences, I decided to volunteer my experience with the wolf. I elaborated on all that my mind's eye perceived.

"Ahh yes, I love that," Mrs. Pittilla began, "the wolf is very strong and wise; a wonderful teacher. You embraced fear and acknowledged wisdom. You are learning, and if you continue to surrender to that process, you will be presented with great teachers."

Mrs. Pittilla continued addressing each step in the meditation, receiving volunteers to share their experiences. The mountains in our visions were composed of all terrains, from soft and plushy to glass. Covered in grass, flowers, snow, and critters. But the enchanting goblet holding the mysterious liquid ended up being the hot topic of the guided meditation.

A student was sharing their experience, "I picked up the goblet and examined it, but I did not drink from it."

"NO!" Mrs Pittilla all but shouted, "The *only* right answer for this step was to drink from the goblet."

Another raised their hand, "What if I inhaled it?" That's what I did, too.

"NO! You needed to drink from it!" Mrs. Pittilla cried.

"What if-"

"No, incorrect," Mrs. Pittilla lamented.

We the students giggled quietly, as most of us it seemed had not taken the easy route and simply drank from the goblet. We were empaths after all, what would you expect? It's not our nature to take.

When questioned about our method of getting down the mountain, students answered with climbing back down the other side, an escalator that led to the bottom, and even helicopters.

"Nope!" Mrs. Pittilla shouted. "The use of vehicles means that you didn't take enough away from the hard and arduous journey you went on."

At that point, I was too scared to share my experience of rising high into the air and expanding my light. I don't like being wrong, though something told me that my experience was more positive than negative.

When we had concluded the group conversation on our meditation experiences, we took a lunch break. Which couldn't have come quick enough because, as is my nature, I was hungry. Over a very healthy and delicious light lunch of soup and salad my momma and I got to know many of the other students. All from different backgrounds and levels of expertise, each one just as receptive as the next to what Mavis Pittilla was sharing with us. Oddly enough, most of the students participating in the workshop held professions in the medical field. My momma included, and myself partly as I was studying psychology. It's not entirely shocking though. Those in the medical field have a knack and desire for helping others, and helping others goes hand in hand with empathy. Empathy, being a pretty important criteria for those participating in psychic/mediumistic workshops.

After lunch, we jumped right back into being as productive as possible, trying to make the most of the two-day workshop that was already zooming by fast. Mavis Pittilla educated us on her psychic techniques, utilizing a powerpoint and everything. We would soon be split into small groups with others who shared the same level of experience. Thankfully this meant I'd be practicing putting my psychic abilities to the test with other beginners. Before we grouped up, Mavis Pittilla shared her technique of connecting with others on a psychic level. It's a personal experience, she explained, and one that should only be done with the purest intentions.

As that responsibility was reinforced in each of us, we picked up our chairs and circled up in our groups. There were five of us in my group. Four women and one man. I knew immediately who I would be able to pick up information on and who I simply would not. In some manner, I resonated with the man and a woman to my left. I took this to mean that we three shared similar demeanors and personalities. For some reason, I was more receptive to their energies. And as it turned out, all three of us were more receptive to each other's energy than to others in the group. To practice our psychic abilities, each person in the group took a turn sitting in the middle of the circle. For ten minutes, each group member would attempt to connect to the life of the individual in the middle, and silently write down whatever came to mind. At the conclusion of the ten minutes, we would go around in a circle sharing and comparing what we picked up on. The individual in the middle would either confirm or deny, sometimes offering details and slight connections.

    I was the first to sit in the middle. A willing and receptive pupil, ready to build some confidence or crush some egos. To the surprise of many of my group members, some valid information was picked up on. I enjoyed being able to confirm the information that came to them. Yes, I spent a lot of time playing soccer throughout middle and high school. Yes, I did have one older brother. Yes, I was single. And yes everyone picked up on that. Thank you everyone for reminding me, I had almost *forgotten*.

    Once the group concluded sharing the information they gathered on me, it was time for another to take my place in the center of the circle. I was ready. I was antsy to connect. To challenge my abilities and see what I could pick up. The man took my place in the center and spent ten minutes meditating while we quietly, yet intensely scrutinized. I filled a notebook page with anything and everything that came to mind. Little random potential facts, experiences he may have had, injuries, places he'd traveled, names, dates, and so forth. I felt as though I wasn't simply creating nonsense in my mind, but rather that I was receiving and therefore creating a transcript. It came time to share, to be confirmed or denied. I prefaced my sharing with the typical "I'm a beginner so take it easy on me" statement, and then I offered what I picked up. Quietly at first.

    "You have one sibling," I stated, only because Mavis Pittilla told us we needed to be confident in our deliveries.

    The man replied, "Yes."

    Phew. 1/1. Good start. I continued on.

    "You have a sister."

"Yes," the man confirmed.

"She is older than you."

The man nodded his head, once again confirming. My fear was quickly dissipating. This was basic information, and could be easily guessed, but the validation at the beginning of my sharing helped me to gain the confidence to continue on with a stronger resolve.

By the end of my list, I was pleasantly surprised and proud of myself to find I had been correct in about 80% of what I wrote down. Although that wasn't my experience for everyone in the group that I attempted to read. I only had that kind of luck with the man and the woman that I felt an immediate connection with. For the other two women, I only picked up a few tidbits of information. The group readings were a challenge that left me exhausted. I felt like I had just ran ten miles. I needed an ice cold Sprite and a bed to pass out in. And other than the feeling of progression and expansion, I experienced an epiphany. This was what I needed! Absolutely. It was obvious once it dawned on me, and yet beforehand it was elusive. Thus far in my journey of spiritual expansion, I'd only been surrounded by experts. My momma, though a great teacher, was beyond me. It had been so long since she was a beginner that she simply couldn't relate as easily with me. All of the well-known authors and mediums and scientists and TV personalities that I looked up to were professionals. I had been judging my abilities and my experiences based off of people I put up on pedestals. No *wonder* I lacked confidence. In this setting, I had the opportunity to work with other curious individuals who were on the same journey as me currently. There was no pressure to be perfect or to get it right even fifty percent of the time. There was only the demand to try and learn and continue forward, in whatever form that happened to be. A few times when my momma had invited close friends over to offer them readings, she'd invite me to sit in and listen. Sometimes she'd look at me and question whether I had picked up messages or information. Timidly, I'd offer a notion that quickly popped into my head. Just as quickly, that notion would be shot down, invalidated. And so went my confidence, knocked down a peg. I'd take on the role of mute bystander once again while my momma worked away, and when she got real into the reading I'd quietly sneak back to hide in my room. So while I was always grateful to be allowed in, it wasn't the kind of space I needed. I needed to be surrounded by mistakes and connection and no expectations.

We were dismissed shortly after the conclusion of the group readings. With the remaining energy I had left, I rambled excitedly to my momma about my experience. But when my butt fell into the front seat of the car, I conked out hard. Soon enough my momma was pulling into our driveway. I had a seatbelt imprint on my cheek. The very same cheek that would soon be diving into a comfy pillow in no longer than five minutes.

My mom and I woke up bright and early again the next morning, this time making a very necessary detour for some gas station coffee. Day two of the workshop was dedicated to our mediumistic abilities, and we needed all of the extra energy we could get.

Everyone exchanged excited conversation on the second day of the workshop. I drank about four cups of coffee in the span of an hour so I was on another level. But the shaking and foot tapping and incessant fidgeting was derailed shortly after the start of class by what Mavis Pittilla called a "discipline". Which for me is just another name for meditation, although I had never done this type before. We the students sat once again upright and determined, receptive and calm in our chairs as Mavis Pittilla guided us through the meditation. We were spending time focusing on each one of the seven main chakras, or energy centers, that ran down the center of our body, beginning with the root chakra located at the base of the spine.

"See the red energy center. Envision it growing in size, expanding. See it swirling. See it connecting with the spirit world. What is two now becomes one. Allow it to continue to spin and expand as we move on to the next chakra. Your sacral chakra, located just below your navel."

At each chakra, we imagined the respective color expanding in size and spinning like a vortex. The goal was to get each chakra moving, connecting with the spirit world. I could envision each of the chakras, bright and spinning, meshing, becoming one with a place that vibrated differently than where I sat physically.

"Now imagine your blue throat chakra spinning and connecting with the spirit world," Mavis Pittilla instructed. I complied, envisioning this union between my throat chakra and the spirit world. And as I did this, I became overwhelmed immediately. My eyes remained shut, but I felt as though hoards of people were now surrounding me. I expected to open my eyes and see faces only centimeters away from me. Suddenly I was claustrophobic. But I breathed deeply and continued forward, surrendering to the unfamiliar feeling of authentically connecting to the spirit world. When we reached the third eye chakra next, I had a greater sense of awareness. Mavis Pittilla continued to talk us through the discipline of strengthening our third eye chakra.

"At this point, dealing with the chakra of intuitive sight, you may see particular spirits or guides coming into your mind's eye. Allow this to happen. If they have messages to share, take it all in."

Mavis Pittilla remained silent for a few minutes to allow any visitors to pop in. I experienced quick flashes of faces that I expected to come forward. My Grandpa Russell, my Grandma Halfmann, and my dog Scoobert Cornellius Doo Russell. They came and went, appearing only briefly to reassure me that they were somewhere nearby supporting me in my quest for spiritual expansion. I smiled back both mentally and physically, just to make sure they knew with 100% certainty that the message was received. And then I both mentally and physically smacked myself upside the head because of course they knew, for I was only a silly human at the moment and they were existing in a much more conscious and connected form than I could even begin to comprehend. It's funny that we humans believe ourselves to be the most intelligent beings, but that's an entirely different topic that deserves its very own book. Back on topic, I was happy to get a quick glimpse at the souls who I knew from this current lifetime as my grandpa, grandma, and favorite doggo. But just as I thought the quick flashes of faces had "de"-ceased (haha, morbid joke), I was surprised by a vivid profile that I would not have expected at that moment. It was a man's face, who I innately knew to be from ancient Egypt. He wasn't sporting the fancy gold head-dress that was commonly associated with the time, and his head wasn't that of a falcon or a large cat or a crocodile. But the man was from the time period of ancient Egypt, and of that I was certain.

"*Who are you?*" I asked internally, to which I received no reply. The mystery lives on. Perhaps he was a guide of mine. That's the explanation I resonate with the most. I've always had a deep affinity for ancient Egypt. A lot of my art projects in school revolved around ancient Egyptian culture. A shelf in my room is solely dedicated to books on the same topic. One of my favorite movies is The Mummy, starring Brendan Fraser. And yes, I do believe that higher beings helped construct the pyramids. Of that I will not be swayed.

The images came and went, as did our focus on the third eye chakra.

Finally, we reached the crown chakra at the very top of our heads. At this point I felt attached to nothing and connected to everything. Where did Morgan begin and where did she end? Was Morgan even real anymore? Was my physical body still there, in that room, sitting on that chair? Or was I simply energy now? Returning to the all? Connecting eternally to everything? Well, I wasn't that far gone apparently because Mavis Pittilla only had to call us to slowly open our eyes and I realized I still had full control of my skin and bones vessel. Unfortunate. I thought I was being pulled to the singularity, which is a term I heard first from my friend after her experiences with psychedelics. Something about ego death and losing touch with individuality and becoming part of the whole. It sounded nice.

My eyes were open though I still felt a sleepiness that goes hand in hand with meditation. But this "discipline" had me feeling not entirely present in the very physical room, filled with other students who were very likely feeling the same lightness. If a gentle gust of wind snuck in through an open window, I'm sure I would have been swept away. And if I wanted to, I'm entirely sure that my astral body could have stepped out from my physical body at that very moment. But I was in that very light state for a purpose, or her name wasn't Mavis Pittilla, goddammit! Or more appropriately, bloody hell! I needed to focus.

But how could I focus when my physical body would not stop twitching? Somewhere along the discipline, I picked up twitching that had my limbs obviously flailing for no reason. During the discipline, I could ignore it and appreciate it as a part of the process. It was like hypnosis. With each twitch of my body, I was falling deeper and deeper. But now that my eyes were opened, and so were everyone else's, the twitching was more obvious and more obnoxious.

Mavis Pittilla was asking about our experiences, allowing those who felt compelled to share. My momma had a heartwarming exchange with her grandmother, my great-grandmother. Another woman saw a familiar spirit guide. And I could not stop *twitching*. So when Mavis Pittilla asked the room if we had any questions about the experience, I raised my hand.

"I cannot stop twitching," I began, "I've experienced this before in deep meditations and am not sure what to make of it. Does anyone else experience twitching?" I looked around to see some nodding heads.

"It's completely natural and part of the growing process. Sometimes twitching is a result of nerves, but I don't sense nerves with you at all. I think it's just your physical body's natural process of opening up and connecting to a different vibration. Energy is flowing in a more intentional way. As you continue your spiritual expansion, it'll occur less and less," Mavis Pittilla smiled at me and continued answering questions for the rest of the students.

"Now that you're all light and only half here, I think it's time for a smoke break!" Mavis Pittilla laughed.

During this break, I decided some non-caffeinated green tea would be good for me.

Fifteen minutes later, we were back in our seats watching as Mrs. Pittilla pulled three chairs to the front of the room.

No, absolutely not. I *refuse*.

"Alright, we're going to have some fun now," Mavis proclaimed, clapping her hands together.

The room buzzed with nervous and excited energy. Mine was just nervous energy. No longer was I excited. Mavis Pittilla explained that now we would be putting what we learned into action; taking turns standing before the class and attempting to connect with the spirit world.

"I am not requiring you to come and stand before the class, especially the beginners." Phew, that was me. She was talking to me.

"I always dreaded public speaking. I wasn't any good at it either. I still don't think I'm a great public speaker, but years of being in the public and speaking have gotten me to where I am now."

She continued on, "this is an opportunity for you to practice platform mediumship in a safe space. You won't be judged. At least not the beginners," she winked at us then.

"This is an opportunity for those of you who feel compelled to come up and give it a try. Don't think about how scary it is to get up and speak in front of people; how scary it is to be wrong. You are learning."

Oh no. Where was she going with this? I didn't like it.

"Don't think about the public speaking part of it. If you think about that, you'll more than likely convince yourself not to come up and give it a try. Rather, ask if your *soul* feels compelled to come up here and practice platform mediumship. If you have any push to come up here, then you owe it to the divine essence within you to *do it*."

Man. Now I had to give it a try. I owed it to my very being and all that jazz. I couldn't hide in my insecurity any longer. I couldn't hide from myself. So I sat there in that moment and let Mrs. Pittilla's speech stew inside me. In the time that I was contemplating her words and arguing with myself, she had chosen three beginners to take the stage. My momma was nudging me, but I felt rushed to volunteer so I waited. Anyways, I *was* the youngest one there. I had nothing to prove, and I'd have plenty more opportunities at plenty more workshops to embarrass myself in *plenty* of ways. My soul could deal with being a bystander for now, I suppose.

Mavis Pittilla shone the spotlight on one person at a time. The object was to connect with a spirit, or sometimes two, gather evidence relating to the spirit, and make a connection to someone in the class that the spirit was associated with. Mavis Pittilla explained that the spirit world planned in advance for these kinds of lessons, so everyone who volunteered would undoubtedly connect with a spirit that had some sort of connection to another student in the room. Furthermore, everyone that connected with a spirit was destined to connect with a specific spirit. How cool is that?

The practice was all about providing clear evidence and validation in a responsible manner. We wouldn't be delivering messages. If messages needed to come through, Mavis Pittilla would rightly take over.

And the first woman was off. Mavis Pittilla grabbed the woman's shoulders and led her to the center of the stage.

"I'm going to connect with your energy to give you a jumping off point," Mavis Pittilla explained, "I'll be feeding you psychic energy to help you connect quicker. To gain that initial confidence."

The woman timidly began, "I think I'm picking up on a man?"

"NO!" Mrs. Pittilla snapped, "Be confident. You either are or you aren't picking up on a man. Be confident before you share."

The woman began again, "I am picking up on a man."

"Good, good," Mavis Pittilla whispered cajolingly. One hand was still wrapped around the woman's shoulder, while her other hand was feeding the woman with psychic energy through her back.

The woman went on to provide more simple details. But details that eventually elicited a connection with one particular student in the room. After the woman had provided four pieces of information, Mavis Pittilla cut her off and looked to the audience to see if the information resonated with anyone. A few hands shot up. We were only supposed to say "yes" if it did, offering no further detail or explanation. As the woman gathered more pieces of information, the hands in the audience decreased until only one student connected with the information.

"Well done!" Mavis Pittilla beamed at the novice. Then the second woman took her place at the center of the stage. The same process ensued, with the same end results. Does it work for everyone? Is it due to Mavis Pittilla's psychic energy magic? I couldn't imagine myself up there, having the same successful experience.

The third woman finally took the stage. She was gentler in her disposition than the other two women. Her movements were graceful. She radiated a very innocent and kind energy that both my momma and I resonated with. We had been pulled to her throughout the workshop for some reason. I thought her to be the brunette version of my momma.

Mavis Pittilla encouraged her to open up and begin. The woman breathed deeply and closed her eyes. She connected.

And who she connected with was a beautiful being who came through for me. The connection couldn't have been a fabrication, for all of the detail and clarity that was provided by this supposedly novice medium. My mom and I knew immediately that the spirit coming through was showing up for us. And it became clear that the spirit was cheering me on in particular, coming through to inspire me with courage to step up and give it the old college try. If this spirit hadn't come through, I likely wouldn't have felt divine pressure to put myself out there like the rest of the class. And though I want nothing more than to honor this messenger who came through with unconditional love and support, I understand that it is not the right time for me to share more information than I already have. I will hold this secret, their identity, until it's time to tell.

I cried tears of happiness and overwhelm throughout the connection. Mavis Pittilla hopped onto the call with the spirit to provide more information when the woman who originally connected stopped receiving. And when Mavis Pittilla concluded, I sighed wishing I had taken the opportunity to practice up in the front and make my messenger proud, but recognizing that the opportunity had come and gone. Darn... next time, Universe!

But the Universe is crafty. It's running the show, always. And it had an accomplice that day in the form of a sassy British woman.

Mavis Pittilla smiled out at us knowingly, "let's actually bring up one or two more beginners if there are any that changed their mind and would like to give it a shot!"

No time to think. My hand shot up. Mavis Pittilla pulled me up to the front. It all happened so fast, I think I blacked out a little. And then there I was, standing before the rest of the students, acting as though I had the potential to do an ounce of justice to the idea of mediumship; to the spirit world. Mavis Pittilla's hands were holding me sturdy in place. She could sense my nerves and instructed me to breathe deeply. To step into my power.

One deep breath. Two deep breaths. And then I felt the power within my reach, so I embraced it by taking that metaphorical step. It was a monumental moment in my spiritual journey, so I likened it to a giant leap. One small step for Mavis Pittilla, one giant leap for Morgan. A shift happened. It was slight and not entirely confident, but enough to encourage me to look up at the audience with conviction, trust, and authenticity.

"Now that you're in your power," Mavis Pittilla explained, "allow the connection to be made with the spirit world. When you feel a connection, you may begin sharing."

At this point Mavis Pittilla placed one palm on my back, and shared psychic energy with me to assist in the initial discernment process. The power grew as I continued to breathe deeply and attempted to connect. I felt more secure now standing in front of the room. The unnerving feeling of eyes on me lessened while the feeling of purpose intensified. And suddenly, I knew I had a man with me. So I said it, boldly. Unquestioningly.

"I have a man with me."

"Yes," Mavis Pittilla whispered from behind me.

I started automatically pulling some Momma moves. Waiting for more information to come to me, I had my hands shoulder width apart, palms facing the ceiling. It felt right. And every few seconds, I'd rub my hands together. Soon enough, the information started coming in, in greater detail.

"He's an older man. I'm getting grandfather level."

Mavis Pittilla prodded me further, "What does he look like?"

I focused. The visual was completely in my mind's eye. This man didn't appear before my physical eyes. I simply knew.

"He is dressed in a plain white t-shirt, tucked into his jeans. A little bit of a belly, but otherwise pretty skinny. Average height."

"Brilliant," Mavis Pittilla whispered from behind me. *The* Mavis Pittilla just told me my mediumship skills were *brilliant*. I saved that experience in the 'important memories' section of my brain for a rainy day.

"Does anyone resonate with this man yet?" Mavis Pittilla questioned the audience.

Many hands shot up to my relief. Although, at that point in gathering information I'm sure most people in the room could resonate with a similar description.

I continued. More information was coming in. Up until this point I had only picked up snippets of information, usually when I wasn't looking for them. But now, it was knowledge gathered intentionally from my array of clairsenses.

"He had something to do with cars or vehicles. I see him working on cars, being greasy. He's sliding under a car with tools in his hand," I started involuntarily mimicking the movements of using a steering wheel. That's clair-sentience, or clear feeling. Feeling pain or illness, emotions, and taking on the physical movements of a spirit.

I kept driving that invisible car, searching around the audience to see if I was pulled in a certain direction as to who might be connected with the spirit.

"Anything else specifically about the vehicle?" Mavis Pittilla prodded.

I paused for a moment, "He worked on vehicles a lot... But he was a truck driver!"

Mavis Pittilla cut me off again, "Does someone still resonate with this information?"

We looked out to the audience, Mavis Pittilla knowing and me crossing my fingers. A woman in the back raised her hand. The only hand left in the room. How I had actually done what the others did was beyond me. It had to have been the magic psychic energy that Mavis Pittilla infused me with. But in reality, I had never put myself in a position such as that before. I had never taken myself seriously enough. At that point, Mavis Pittilla asked if I had more to offer. Nothing was coming to me.

With a big ole smile, she congratulated me on my first platform mediumship experience. Gently she directed me back to my seat in the audience, and continued her assessment of my work as she had done with the others after every connection.

"You are very powerful in your delivery, very confident. You need to continue platform mediumship. Practicing in the comfort of your home with books isn't going to be beneficial for you at this point. Does that make sense? You need to practice in public with real people."

Gulp. Drag me, Mavis Pittilla. I *was* very comfortable with my books.

The workshop had me on a high for weeks to follow. A renewed sense of purpose was instilled in me once more. A fresh wave of motivation washed over me. And yet, I was still not entirely satisfied. What was it going to take, Morgan? Would I ever be fully satisfied? I know my family needed to know for their sanity! But it was clear to me that the 180's, characterized by new lessons and learning, were quintessential to my journey through this lifetime. And as they say, it's not about the destination, it's about the journey.

So at this point, I was learning and putting what I learned into action and growing and manifesting and really working on awareness. But beyond all of that, I was *itchy*. Itchy from the stagnation that I seemed to happen upon often. How was that possible when I was constantly on the move? Never in one place for too long. Never committing to one thing for a considerable period of time. I was never passionate or satisfied with a job enough to stick around. The same with cities, houses, environments. And it's not for lack of discipline. Somewhere deep inside my soul I knew that I was on a quest to discover more facets of myself, and I would not feel a sense of excitement for life if I wasn't honoring that knowledge. The Universe knew exactly how to get me from one place to the other, and it manifested in the form of restlessness. So, as is my nature, I decided to switch it up once more. This time, on a greater scale. It was time yet again to do a 180 with my life; to become comfortable with the uncomfortable. How will Morgan shift her reality next? Stay tuned. Like The Magician in the tarot, I always have something up my sleeve.

♡ Chapter 9 ♡

Not Today, Satan... ergh, Sun Devil's?

    I travel with a backpack. Always. There's never a time that you'll find me without a backpack. At this point in my life, it's an extension of my physical body complete with an aura and everything. I bring that backpack everywhere, packed with the necessities. My toothbrush, a change of clothes, my tarot cards. The usual. Anyone who knows me, knows I come and go like the wind. Maybe even more frequently. I'm in a constant state of change, with every aspect of my life. But as I've said, it's within that state that I feel most alive. From an early age I've been on the move. I've lived in more houses growing up than I can count on my fingers. And there was nothing that made me more excited than packing my room up into boxes, except unpacking those boxes in a new place, of course. And when I got a car, I would drive myself and my dog, Scooby, back and forth between my momma's house and my dads. Scooby rode shotgun as we meandered the roads of Marinette County. The windows rolled down, a fresh breeze slinging the drool off of Scooby's chops. We were a singular, fleeting moment and infinite all at once. Maybe that constant coming and going played a role in my affinity for change. Maybe it was preparing me for a future of going and exploring.

    So I travel with a backpack, never staying in one place for too long. It's my nature. I am nothing if not a Sagittarius, and I take a great deal of my pride in my sun sign.

    One random day as it always is, I had an epiphany. Here I was, young and able-bodied, doing my undergrad online, in between jobs, and independent, yet feeling extremely stagnant and *bored*. It was time for a major change. A more opportune time hadn't existed thus far, and I'd be damned if I was going to acknowledge it and just let it pass me by without taking any kind of action. My horoscope apps even agreed, confirming that I was about to undergo a major life transformation. I was going to finally put my transient lifestyle to better use, on a much grander scale. I was going to move out of my parents' houses for good. But it wouldn't be your average everyday move. It needed to be wild and new, limitless and free. It needed to shake up my being and set in motion an entirely new dynamic. What's the opposite of Wisconsin?

Arizona, my analytical mind and higher self responded simultaneously. Likely the first time those two entities were ever in agreement. That answer didn't come out of nowhere. It had been a dream of mine from a young age, though I hadn't ever given it the consideration that I was giving it at that particular moment. If you looked at one of my vision boards, you would see *Arizona* tacked up at the very top of my list of travel destinations. A goal. When I was young, I would imagine wandering the deserts and traversing the massive rocks. A daydream. When I was applying for colleges, I researched in Arizona. An impractical concept. Divine timing had kept me at a distance from that place. Still, I continued to hold it close through the years. But perhaps the Universe was opening a doorway at this very moment and inviting me in. All was aligning in the physical world, encouraging something great to transpire.

Queue the ego, crashing the party.

"How are you going to make that happen? Why would you think that you could do something like that? You wouldn't be safe. You would fail. It would be a mistake," the voice in my head called to me. But Arizona called to me louder. It became harder to ignore. There were signs constantly showing up in my life. Signs that were the equivalent of taking a blow horn to my ear and shouting "ARIZONA, BABY!"

TV shows that I watched would take place in Arizona. *Grey's Anatomy* introduced Arizona Robbins to the show around the same time. I had never heard of someone named Arizona, but there she was in all of her fictional PhD glory. I was seeing Arizona license plates all over the place in Wisconsin. For example, when I was helping my bestie, Noah, move apartments, the U-Haul we used had an Arizona license plate. After calling my momma to tell her about it, she excitedly explained that she was currently in the car, driving behind a van with an Arizona plate. A few days later, my dad and my stepmom took my stepsister and I to a baseball game to watch Yelich add another home-run to his record. Go Brewers! To my surprise, they were playing the Arizona Diamondbacks. A couple days later, a friend showed me a song called *Sedona*. These little coincidental happenstances kept on coming, and I became increasingly aware of them. But I don't believe in coincidences. Per the Law of Attraction, the more I focused on these signs for Arizona, the more they turned up around me. Sure, maybe it was my brain's astute ability to recognize patterns, or maybe it was the Universe giving me validation to a potential path I'd embark on. I was caught up somewhere in the middle of those two ways of thinking. Not convinced yet, but not-*not* convinced.

    I remembered back a few weeks earlier to the guided meditation Mavis Pittilla led all the students in the workshop through. What type of terrain had I seen in my mind's eye? Dusty, dry, red rock. The very same dusty, dry, red rock that Arizona was known for. And remembering that previously unnoticed clue into my future led me to remember a reading from a year prior that also resonated with the idea of Arizona. The psychic had me pick a small magnet from a bowl, eyes closed. I plucked out a tiny picture of dry terrain and red rocks. In small letters, it read *The Spirit of Place*. The psychic told me the imagery resonated with me, but I thought she was fibbin. I was a water and grass kind of girl, through and through. A year later and I'm thinking maybe she was onto something. That same magnet found a place stuck to my bookshelf, right next to my bed for the months to come. For a year, I saw that magnet just about everyday. A clue from the Universe about my future? A tool for manifestation? Either way, the idea of Arizona became more and more real and, looking back, I saw how often it had popped in waiting for acknowledgement. Little breadcrumbs from the Universe.

    In a short span of time, my thoughts flipped from "I could go to Arizona" to "I'm *going* to Arizona." I preached to everyone the idea of each of us having the capacity to create our realities, so it was time I fully sent it. One night with a glass of wine in hand and change on my mind, I decided to take to the internet. It was my initial intention that I would make a very short, and very cheap, trip to Arizona to ascertain whether or not I liked the place *at all*. I had only briefly been to Arizona when my family drove from Las Vegas to the Grand Canyon for all of one hour. I spent most of the car ride sleeping, too.

    Cheap. How could I make this trip cheap?

    Hostels. Yes, hostels. Excellent idea, Morgan.

    Thanks, Morgan.

    Something about the idea of hostels always made me excited. Cool people. Lots of culture. Giant slumber party. So I searched for hostels in Arizona and stumbled across a beautiful gift from the Universe. The first choice on Trip Advisor was Phoenix

Hostel and Cultural Center, so I clicked on the webpage. I was redirected to a colorful display with a large notification in the middle of the screen that could not be missed.

"NOW HIRING VOLUNTEERS FOR NOVEMBER AND BEYOND."

So tipsy me did as tipsy me does: shrugged noncommittally and went for it. Redirected by a click once again, I was now presented with an application. Question after question, I answered.

It was never in my plan to volunteer at a hostel, but it quickly became something that I wanted more than anything. When I first started at college, I planned on majoring in anthropology or international studies or history. Something that would allow me to study cultures, whether past or present. That was my passion before I realized that I could maybe, possibly, potentially have a career centered around my ever-expanding spirituality. Not to mention, like most, I always envisioned myself road tripping across the United States or backpacking across Europe. Those visions always included hostels.

And I knew I was going to be offered a position to volunteer. I *knew* it. It wasn't questionable in my mind. It was real and imminent. I kept that stubborn mentality and flew with it. I planned the next couple of months with the hostel smack dab in the center of every possible path. I told everyone around me that I was moving to Arizona to volunteer at a hostel, like it was already my reality because, intuitively, I knew it was. So when I got a reply back from the hostel operations manager requesting a video call interview with me, it was only protocol to me, *knowing* I'd be welcomed at the hostel soon.

And when they confirmed that I had received the volunteer/work exchange position, I did a quick high-five with the Universe and started packing immediately. The Universe works in mysterious (but not surprising, at this point) ways. Once I put my intentions into getting to Arizona, the wheels of *flow* were set in motion.

Everything was happening fast. I wanted to get to Arizona *fast*. Faster than felt right, to be honest, but staying in Wisconsin any longer felt wrong. I wanted to be in Sedona, Arizona, basking in the energy vortexes that the city was so popular for. I wanted to bump by happenstance into Drunvalo Melchizedek and chat about our infinite existence over a glass of celery juice. I wanted to be somewhere new, with unknown, exciting experiences before me and the stagnancy that characterized my life left in the past.

The hostel wanted me to start at the beginning of November, which was one and a half months away. To me, this was less than ideal. Things were not happening on the surface the way I had hoped they would. I was living back at home, in both Marinette and Coleman, without a job after living in Madison for a few short summer months. It didn't feel ideal to me, having to start a job again for the duration of 1 and a half months, only to leave once more. So I kept trying to make the plan inside my head work. I researched airbnb's all over Arizona, looking for cheap places to rent for an entire month. The plan was that I would rent a place for a month in Phoenix, Arizona, and I'd immediately find a part-time job before I began volunteering at the hostel. This would give me time to acclimate to the area, find a side-hustle, and be out of Wisconsin as soon as I'd hoped.

There were many options for renting, but for the first couple of days I could not get myself to click the "commit" button. My hands would not allow it. Do it, dammit! But to no avail. Over the following days, the options for renting began to dwindle. Frazzled, I picked one of the last available places and decided to run with it. I plugged in my debit card information to book the reservation, but as the Universe would have it, my debit card was declined for the order. Try as I might, the reservation wouldn't go through. That's fine. That's real fine. I'll just move on to the *next* available option. But when I attempted to make a reservation again, the host declined my booking. They saw my reservation request and immediately took their location offline. Intimidated by all 5 foot 3 of me, understandably. At this point I was frazzled and annoyed and *over it*. I slammed my laptop shut, huffing and puffing over the way things were unfolding - not well, to my limited understanding. What was I doing wrong? Wasn't I supposed to go to Arizona? Wouldn't it make more sense to proceed in the way I intended to, Universe? That's when I recognized that things often do not make sense in the perspective of the critical mind, at least where the Universe is involved. Where did I get off thinking that a feeble, human mind like mine had a greater understanding of the ebb and flow of what was to come? I was forcing the plan, when I should have been letting it unravel with an equal measure of both inspired planning and simply surrendering control.

"PATIENCE BE DAMNED," I was saying.

"Ha!" the Universe retorted, "I guess we'll see about that..."

It was unrealistic that I keep on in the way that I was moving, with lodging a complete bust. So I let my need for complete control go after a deep inhale of acceptance and a long exhale of surrender.

"Alright, you win. YOU WIN! I will be patient!" I shouted, fist shaking at the sky.

It was apparent that I needed to be patient. To plan and to prepare. To be more realistic instead of head-in-the-clouds Morgan as per usual. And that's a difficult transition for me, whose being is synonymous with "impractical". I thought that quality was part of my charm, but perhaps it was my fatal flaw; my hamartia, if you will. Quickly, I was cajoled by this metaphorical wall I had hit to understand that everything requires balance in this duality-based world.

So as the Universe would have it, I decided I would focus on saving money for a bit by living at home, waiting for the more practical time to make my move; waiting for when it flowed easily. I would wait until I could move directly into the hostel to volunteer, instead of paying for a month of rent at an airbnb. I'm sure the Universe held a collective slow clap for me once I made that decision to surrender. The Universe knew all along. Once I released my self-imposed timeline, the Universe could breathe again. And so could I, finally, without constriction. That decision happened around 11pm one night, and the very next morning the hostel reached out to me.

"One of our volunteers is actually moving out sooner than we thought. Any chance you'd be able and willing to start as early as October 1st?"

Are you kidding me? Was it truly that easy? I had spent one too many days stressing and attempting to construct a path that would unfold *effortlessly* if I just allowed it. Surrender is the perfect embodiment of easy to preach yet difficult to practice per our analytical minds. But the result is worth it. That mysterious Universe is always ten steps ahead, and then some. Will I learn that lesson quicker next time instead of struggling for control as long as possible? Stay tuned.

The plan was activated. The path was being illuminated before me. Now all I could do was wait, and use the few weeks of free time to prepare for the move. After the initial blind excitement wore off, it turns out I could also use that free time to worry endlessly. One night I found myself anxiously and obsessively shuffling my tarot cards, like a nervous tick. I paced around the house shuffling until I decided to pull a card. Arizona was happening fast and reality was setting in.

One more shuffle for good luck, and I plucked a single card from the deck. A spooky man in a grey cloak, holding a lantern before him. The Hermit. What a wonderful sign from the Universe. The Hermit represents a spiritual journey, whether physical or not. In my case, physical and non-physical. I was the Hermit, indubitably. And for some reason, I felt compelled to pull another card. The Fool. Another major arcana card. This card represented new beginnings of innocence and spontaneity. The resonation was real. Two major arcana cards that I was embodying to a tee. My anxiety was quelled for a hot second, renewed with a sense of confidence. Seeing The Fool led me to another, more detailed reading, out of simple curiosity, in search of further reassurance. The particular reading entails pulling The Fool from the deck, as well as twelve randomly selected cards. Those thirteen cards are shuffled every which way and eventually laid out in a straight, horizontal line. A timeline. The Fool is meant to symbolize yourself presently. Therefore, the cards that come before the Fool speak on your past experiences and obstacles whereas the cards that follow tell of what's to come. If The Fool appears towards the beginning, most of your journey is still ahead. If The Fool appears towards the end, your particular journey is winding down. I picked out my twelve additional cards and mixed in the Fool, along with some good intentions. Vigorous shuffling ensued, and then I laid the cards out before me. My momma was watching on at this point.

"The Fool is going to be at the very beginning," I explained, knowing for about 98% certainty that it was true. I flipped the first card and, low and behold, was staring at The Fool once more.

And so it seemed that everything was yet to come, as was expected. The cards depicted highs and lows, which is not surprising in the slightest considering life on Earth is one proverbial rollercoaster until we croak, or attain complete enlightenment I suppose. And in reading the cards, it would appear that I was at the very beginning of a new journey, jumping spontaneously into the unknown, as is The Fool's nature. I knew The Fool would come first in the spread, because I knew that I was only on the precipice of understanding what's to be understood and learning what's to be learned in regard to my spiritual expansion. Perhaps The Fool will always show up as the first card in all my attempts at that type of reading. A reminder that I'll be in a constant state of learning, as it should be, with more always to come. Learning will be eternal, just like our souls. And just like the wait for Arizona. Though strictly in a metaphorical sense, because soon enough I was saying goodbye to my wonderful animals, giving each a kiss and a boop on the head, and rolling my suitcase out the door.

      On the drive to the airport, I silently ruminated over all of the signs and validation that I'd been given in the buildup to Arizona. A few days prior to leaving, I had a strange experience. Strange being subjective, of course, as all of the signs I've been privy to seem strange in their own right. I was at the gym picking up weights and putting them down when my phone buzzed. A daily notification from one of my favorite horoscope apps popped up on my lock screen. The app sends you short, daily messages to get you thinking, and that day's message read, *"Name something you did that you should be proud of."*

      I didn't have any time to consider this message when another notification popped up on the screen just below. It was a notification from the Notes app, displaying the name of one of my most recent notes, titled *ARIZONA* in all caps. What the - And as quickly as the Note notification titled *ARIZONA* popped up, it disappeared. A notification from the Notes app? I didn't know that was a thing. Was it a glitch? A very, very coincidental glitch then. The likes of which had not happened prior and has not happened since. After a forty minute drive, we rolled up to the drop-off zone at Austin Straubel Airport in Green Bay, Wisconsin.

      The synchronicities and signs ensued, following us on our journey to Arizona, never missing a beat. I had been resonating with the number 2 for a while building up to the epiphany of Arizona, and it only became more prominent in my life the closer I got to my destination. The row our seats were in on the plane was 22. That could be a coincidence, but say it with me. *Coincidences don't exist!* Louder for the people in the back of the plane.

      Our flight had a connection in Denver, so off one plane and onto the next we went. We were seated next to a woman that seemed to be my momma's age. They started talking and, as the Law of Attraction would have it no other way, it turns out she held the same particular perspective on spirituality that my momma and I did. Naturally we'd end up seated by each other on the plane *filled* with diversity. It was a night flight, but my momma and her talked and talked. I couldn't catch much of the conversation because my ears plugged up from the altitude.

      We eventually landed and zombie-walked out of the terminal in a sleepy stupor, only sparing enough energy to hoist our bags from the conveyor belt in passing.

My momma was contacting someone from our hotel to send a shuttle our way when she looked at me and laughed, briefly covering the phone with her hand.

"Our driver's name is Angel," she whispered goofily.

We exited the busy airport and waited for our shuttle by the taxi line-up. I felt the energy of Phoenix buzzing all around me. The night sky, a beautiful contrast against the Uber headlights and neon signs posted around the edge of the airport. Man, the air was so warm it felt like I was in DisneyLand. I really felt like a kid at an amusement park. I wanted to live in that moment forever. My backpack slung over my shoulder. Energy moving and shaking in all directions. Cars zooming by on the ramps high up in the sky and planes floating by even higher yet. And then an angel showed up in white hotel van, ready to escort us further along on our spiritual journey.

Nothing exciting happened that night. It was past midnight before we got settled into our Phoenix hotel room. Spirits had no chance at keeping us awake. We zonked out hard. But not as hard as I went at the continental breakfast the following morning.

My momma and I had the weekend to explore Arizona before she'd drop me off at the hostel on Monday morning. So once I finished shoving toast in my mouth, along with my third cup of coffee, we were off to our first real destination; Sedona.

I've always romanticized Sedona, and for good reason. The beautiful and vast red rocks that look like paintings. The energy vortexes that apparently had the power of being *almost* tangible for *almost* everyone. And Drunvalo Melchizedek lived in Sedona. Need I say more? The drive from Phoenix to Sedona was just under two hours. What started as a trip along flat terrain and tumbleweeds quickly shifted to narrow, winding roads between rocks and along cliffs. Pictures cannot do justice to the ethereal landscape that's been untouched in many parts of Arizona. My momma and I joked that there must be one massive projector doing a hell of a job convincing us of the view. But really we both know that Mother Nature's natural beauty is just something that can't be comprehended too quickly.

Pulling into Sedona had my momma and I "oohing" and "ahhing" as we made it down the main strip. Sure, there were more tourist shops serving aura images and readings and crystals than you could shake a stick at. But it's what's beyond the material and the physical that enraptured us. All the talk about the energy turned out to be real, to our excitement.

Our first day in Sedona was spent driving to scenic spots. Vortexes and views, baby. A sprinkle of good energy here, a dash of sick vantage points there. We were still wiped from the late night travel, so we decided to see the "must-see" spots on a different day once the energy that surrounded us helped to pick us up.

The first day we spent in Sedona was actually the birthday of my Grandma Halfmann, who had passed a couple years prior. Birthdays are always difficult when you lose a loved one, but we knew Grandma Halfmann was with us throughout our journey. Who would pass up on a free trip? So of course she was with us. In fact we know she was. That day we stopped in at a busy restaurant for lunch. Up to the hostess stand we went, eager to claim our buzzer. As we stepped up to the hostess, she yelled out, "Cynthia, party of three!".

"HA!" laughed my momma. The actual party of three for Cynthia got their table, but my momma and I got a cool little message of reassurance from Grandma Cynthia Halfmann.

That first day, I was also gifted with pennies upon pennies. Just more signs to reassure me. That, or the great people of Sedona *literally* had holes in their pockets. I snuck out to an area of artificial turf by the pool and skipped around it while facetiming my bestie, Noah.

"Look at the *views*!" I shouted into the phone, turning the camera to the red rocks right across the street.

"I'm so *happy*!" I shouted into the phone, turning the camera to get a close-up of my pearly whites.

"Who *is she*?" Noah asked in dramatic fashion.

I went on to explain all of the travels up until that point, and all of the signs and validation I had received thus far.

"Pennies," I said to Noah, explaining their mysterious, yet not so mysterious, way of turning up all over the place. And as I was explaining the pennies, I took a step and squished my bare feet into the turf. Something foreign beneath my foot, I felt. Still on the phone with Noah, I lifted it and low and behold, a penny from the Universe. From Grandma Halfmann, Grandpa Russell, and I believe all my other loved ones who are helping to guide me from somewhere extraordinary.

"No. Way. Get this, Noah-"

* * * * *

The first night that we spent at a hotel in Sedona, it was evident that sleep would not come easily. That's typical when you're staying at a hotel, and even more typical for my momma on a daily basis, but this was next-level sleep deprivation. It was 3am, hours after we initially tried to get to sleep. My momma finally decided to turn the TV off and rolled over. I sat up on my phone for another fifteen minutes, and decided to give sleep another shot. I rolled over, closed my eyes, and sighed deeply.

Yes, this was off to a good start. The sleepy's were coming, I could feel it.

And then I felt someone get into bed next to me. I froze for a few seconds, hoping to discover that I was simply kidding myself. Nope. The covers rustled next to me and the mattress dipped like a large human body was snuggling in. I smacked the nightstand light on and started mumbling, "oh no, no, no, no, absolutely NOT, not tonight."

My mom sat up from her sleep. She looked at me like *YIKES*, and I made my way over to her bed, huffing, with my pillow and blanket in hand. I conked out quickly at that point.

And then I woke up the next morning speaking, as I do quite often. Words rambling out of my mouth before I'm even fully conscious.

"Aldous Huxley," I kept mumbling until I became aware of what I was saying.

Aldous who? Aldous Huxley? Never heard of him. But as is my routine when this happens, I immediately typed his name into my notes for safe-keeping and googled him once I woke up enough to use the keyboard on my phone properly.

Aldous Huxley, though previously unknown to me, was both a philosopher and a writer. He wrote on the topic of spiritual ideas such as eastern religions and mysticism, along with Universalism which is the belief that we have a free search for truth and meaning. The belief takes certain universal aspects from many of the most popular religions found around the world.

My eyebrows scrunched tighter with each article I read. How curious that Aldous Huxley, who wrote on those particular topics, would be the name that I spoke myself awake with while in the thick of my physical and non-physical spiritual journey. While in Sedona, a metaphysical hub, no less! How curious that he happened to be an acclaimed writer of spiritual topics when I was hoping to make a dent in that field as well. And how curious the manner was that I was given his name. Perhaps I had seen Aldous Huxley's name and career somewhere in my twenty-plus years, and perhaps my brain held onto that select information for that particular sleepy morning in Sedona, Arizona for no reason at all. Or more likely, in my opinion, it was another sign from the Universe, maybe even Mr. Huxley himself, that my quest for truth and expansion was unfolding perfectly before me.

    Way too soon, it was time to pack up and say goodbye to Sedona. I wanted to stay longer, become more immersed in all that Sedona offered spiritually. In my head I was already overanalyzing my plans and contemplating whether I could get out of the hostel commitment. I really didn't want to leave the red rocks. Sedona felt right. I felt like I was home. I've always wanted to move, move, move, but Sedona, the place that had called to me from some 1800 miles away, made me feel like suddenly I could stay in one place. But Sedona was not in the cards for the time being, and I knew this. As much as I wanted it, I knew it wasn't our time to experience each other fully and deeply. Phoenix, on the other hand, had a lot of plans for me and I, for it.

    Goodbye red rocks. Hello palm trees and highways. An hour and a half later my momma and I were zooming down the busy Phoenix freeway in our rental car, headed to the hostel I'd be calling home for two months. My momma was heavy breathing in the driver's seat, taking in the foreign surroundings. The large and looming buildings. The five-lane highway. The people, the lack of water, the street art, the mountains, the cacti. So much cacti.

    "Breathe, Momma," I whispered, "it's not scary, just new."

    And as it always happens, we were taken aback but not entirely surprised to see a single balloon floating in the middle of the highway as cars zoomed by.

    "Is that a balloon?" I deadpanned.

    "It sure is," my momma replied, visibly relaxing a smidgen.

    Not the best place to present us with a sign, Grandpa, but appreciated nonetheless. Phoenix drivers are already notoriously crazy. Let's not put any more balloons on the highway, yeah?

    Excitement was coursing through me. A new start? My favorite! Being uncomfortable? Embracing the unknown? My specialties! And still a part of me, the very human part of me, was afraid that I had made entirely the wrong choice. That pesky ego! But I was already here, and the path before me had unfolded so effortlessly.

Nothing had ever felt more right. So, I let the Universe carry me forward as my mom dropped me off at the front doors of the hostel.

"It's not scary, just new," I reminded myself, storing the mantra in my mind for all of the experiences to come. How absolutely fitting for a spiritual journey such as this.

♡ Chapter 10 ♡

It's a Dry Heat… But I'm Still So Sweaty :-(

Change is uncomfortable. But I find comfort in the uncomfortable. The first few days at the hostel were a rollercoaster of highs and lows. Highs, because of the people and the constant go, go, go towards new experiences and activities. Lows, for the very same reasons. It was a shock to my system. A system that knew introversion and comfort and monotony. Suddenly I was thrown into meeting a new person with a new perspective every time I stepped out of my room. I was exhausted, in the best way possible, at the end of each day from non-stop exploration and an unreal amount of conversation that I didn't realize I was capable of. My head would hit the pillow, and that was that. I'd wake up in what seemed like seconds to the noisy chatter coming from the common area at breakfast time. On one of the first days, I asked my roommate, Nicole, if the staff ever took naps. Please say yes. Please say yes.

"Of course we take naps," she replied, smirking at me.

"Man, that's good to hear. I thought I was supposed to rally all day everyday!"

She laughed at that, "Sometimes you gotta sneak into your room and just hide for the day to recover energetically."

And on day four, the Universe said, "Let there be naps!" and there were naps. Lots and lots of naps.

Toward the beginning of my stay on a warm night, no different than the rest, our hostel put together a barbecue for the staff and guests complete with veggie brats and burgers. I snuck inside after a short while to get a break from all the energy. Also because I was intermittently fasting, so I needed to *not* be around barbecue food. I would have done questionable things for a veggie burger in the thick of my fast. I was surprised to see a guest had followed me. Turns out we both had the same idea with taking a break from the energy. We bonded over a talk on spirituality and, further, introversion. He spoke some truth about the reality of being an empath-introvert, as we both were. Our energy depleted so much faster than extroverts. Whereas extroverts derive energy from being around others, introverts charge up in solitude.

"This must be very difficult for you, volunteering at the hostel *and* living here at the same time, always around people and shifting energies," the guest acknowledged.

And it was; it challenged me. It was uncomfortable, but that's where growth happens. I felt drained by the end of each day, but I'd wake up each morning more excited to be alive than ever before. In no time at all, I was able to acclimate to the easygoing lifestyle that the hostel was known for. Everyday new guests would introduce themselves, coming and going in a manner that was familiar to me. And hey! They all carried backpacks wherever they went, just like me. My people.

How did I get so lucky to be in a place as cool as this one? The front yard welcomed in all who passed by with bright and beautiful energy. By day, the hostel yard was a lively desert oasis. Birds sang their songs, flowers and cacti existed unapologetically anywhere they could cram in. Music was always playing both inside and outside the hostel. We took turns picking the stations, but it typically sounded like Glass Animals or Pandora's version of a French coffee shop. Guests came and went as they pleased, some choosing to literally hang around in the hammocks and others cramming in cars to hike the highest peaks surrounding Phoenix. The best part was that the hostel bestowed each guest and staff member with the innate ability to find all free experiences near the city, and so we did them all. Museum perusing, niche day-festivals in the downtown parks, dance classes, hikes, wine tasting, poetry slams, and more. It never mattered who joined in. We hailed from different states, countries, and continents. We spoke a slew of languages, and though we couldn't always understand the sentences our words created, we had a mutual understanding. Connection, regardless of everything else. We always found a way around the cultural barriers. Can you imagine that world? It's already existing at the Phoenix Hostel & Cultural Center.

By night, stringed lights twinkled over the yard as guests sprawled out in deep conversation. We might have had the projector on in the front yard, showing a foreign film complete with bean bag chairs, or we may have set up some hors d'oeuvres on the patio table for picking. Indoors, guests and staff connected over cooking in collaboration. Some played the guitars in unison. My second night at the hostel, a group of us packed into the cozy TV room and watched an alien documentary. These really *were* my people. Though there were plenty of options to entertain us guests and staff, each night typically ended with a group seated around the big roundtable that sat in the center of the common area, sharing stories, travel plans, and dreams. I could write another book about all of the things I heard at that table alone. Maybe someday.

    The deal with the hostel was that I had a place to live for free with the agreement that I volunteered around the place usually twenty hours a week. I had a bed, all utilities and necessities, and even food provided for me. It was a dream experience, but that doesn't mean it was always glamorous. Sometimes I had to clean toilets. A few days into my stay and it was my first solo run on the morning cleaning shift. Making beds, vacuuming floors, scrubbing toilets, the works. There I was, on hands and knees scrubbing around a shower drain to work the grime away and pull up all the strands of hair that were accumulating into a small nest. I hope you have a nice visual in your head. Maybe the surface of the shower could use some more cleaning spray? I turned my sight away from the drain for one quick moment to grab the bottle of cleaner, and deadpanned upon turning back and seeing a single penny sitting atop the drain. Where it came from was beyond me. It hadn't been sitting there a second ago. Did I make it clear that I was scrubbing grime and pulling strands of hair from the same drain? The penny hadn't fallen from my pocket. Physics would not permit that to happen in the position I was seated. Furthermore, I hadn't heard a penny drop. So I sent a silent thank you up to my Grandma Halfmann and Grandpa Russell. And then I sent a silent request for quarters instead of pennies, considering how often the coins mysteriously showed up. No harm in asking for a raise, right?

    So it was early October when I took up residence at the Phoenix Hostel and Cultural Center. The most wonderful time of the year, in my opinion. Being in Arizona for October meant that I didn't have to wear a jacket over my Scooby-Doo Halloween costume. Yes, although it was spooky season, it felt like Christmas to me. All of the people and experiences that I crossed paths with were metaphorical presents under a big green Christmas tree. And one of my favorite presents was the Rising Phoenix Spiritualist Church.

    Before I left Wisconsin, I had finished reading Mavis Pittilla's book, *Droplets of God,* and learned much about the Spiritualist Church, which she belonged to most of her life. I hadn't ever heard of spiritualism prior to the workshop, but it soon became both a foundation and catalyst for my personal spiritual expansion. Going to a Presbyterian church as a young girl had a certain way of making me feel light back then, but I didn't always resonate with the teachings. Ultimately, I became apprehensive of church as time went on, knowing that for me it did not resonate with my beliefs and ideas. But because I was so inspired by the momentum of my expansion, and all of the cool facets of the spiritual teachers that I encountered, I let my curiosity propel me forward. I found the Rising Phoenix Spiritualist Church only two miles away from the hostel. Free courses for all experience levels and weekly healing services were offered. So I wrote the dates and times for all of the events in my planner. After all, moving to Arizona had everything to do with my spiritual expansion.

   I had friends from the hostel who were also interested in checking the church out, as the Law of Attraction would have it. So one Sunday we uber'd over for a healing service, which wasn't a service like I'd experienced in the past. The church was based out of a cute little house in a seemingly-normal neighborhood. But inside the house existed a light and powerful energy. One that welcomed us immediately. My fellow hostel volunteer, Benny, two tag-a-long guests, and I ventured in, expecting to listen as a leader spoke on the principles of spirituality. We were surprised to find ourselves in the midst of what seemed like a house-warming party whose theme was energy healing, complete with party favors in the form of small crystals and an email newsletter we could sign up for. This form of service was wonderful news for me and my inability to sit still. A man wandered over to us, smiling, and gave the rundown on what our experience would be like at the church. He explained that four different types of healing services were being offered on that specific day, at no cost, and that we were invited to sign up for any of the services. I wrote my name under "healing circle" and "chakra balance therapy", unsure of what each would entail but pulled to those modalities of healing. Those who came along with me picked sessions that best resonated with them as well. And then we waited for our names to be called.

   In further exploration of the house, we found a small shelf of books available to anyone and a couple trays of finger foods. Naturally I'd find myself amongst the books and the snacks. The Universe would not have it otherwise. Get this girl a book on soulmates and some cauliflower and dip, *pronto!*

   The tag-a-long guests who accompanied Benny and I to the church were both interested in learning more about the spiritualist church. One of the guests was an older lady studying hypnosis. She was staying at the hostel while a hypnosis convention was happening in downtown Phoenix. The first night after I had met her, I dreamt that she hypnotized me. I'm not entirely sure if it was a dream, but I'm going to keep moving forward like it was. She seemed innocent enough and, for once in my life, my fear overrides my curiosity.

At the church, the four of us waited around the trays of food until we were called for our different sessions. I was the last to be called, but I waited patiently by checking out the collection of books. I took one with me at the end of the day, which was encouraged. A book on divine partnerships, because I am a cheeseball and I love love. When I was finally called for my first session, I was directed into a room with natural light shining in through walls of windows, enveloping every corner. I was a little perturbed to see a single chair in the middle, meant for me, surrounded by six or seven women all smiling at me as I walked in. I cautiously sat in the chair in the middle, so far so good, and let them explain the process.

"Hello! We are mediums, psychics, energy healers, etcetera. We are going to work together to hold space for your energy. We'll each work to pick up important messages and information for you. Just take some deep breaths and we'll do the same."

So I did just that, breathed deeply and relaxed into the unfamiliar experience. All it took was a few inhales and exhales in the peace and quiet when the first woman spoke up.

"I'm not receiving any messages from spirit for you today."

That was okay. I hadn't been expecting any messages from my loved ones. They share messages with me everyday in the form of signs, and through my momma who still called me over the phone to share everything she received for me. And at this point in time, I hear their responses myself to the conversations that at one time felt one-sided.

Another woman spoke up.

"You have very strong energy, but the energy on your back is a little weak at the moment. Are you going through a period of transition?"

I explained how I just moved to Arizona from Wisconsin, and shared with the group my new living situation at the hostel.

"Ahh yes," she said, "you are lacking structure, support, at the moment. That makes complete sense. You don't have family here. You are by yourself. I'm going to help clear out the weak energy on your back and replace it with healing, strong energy. You'll be more grounded and have a sturdier foundation to move forward with."

She waved her hands methodically to bring that good, good to my back.

"Thanks!" I said goofily.

Another woman spoke up then.

"You have a lot of energy pooling in and around your head. Do you have psychic abilities?"

"I'm working on it," I replied.

"You are very intelligent," the lady continued.

Who, me? Stop.. But please continue.

"You know and understand the important aspects of spirituality. You read and study and learn more and more everyday as is your way, but I feel like you need to practice these concepts now. You haven't really had a public space to do that, have you?"

I shook my head, no.

"You need to have a space to be able to practice your abilities openly, with other people. A space where you can meditate on these abilities. A space where you can grow in ways you haven't yet. Come to our Tuesday development circle!"

The healing circle was quick and to the point, but effective in inspiring *even more* of a desire to learn and level up. I walked out of the room rocking fresh back energy and had been given the info on how to continue expanding spiritually. I was in and out within five minutes, and shortly after ushered into my next healing session dedicated to balancing my chakras. A woman with beautiful feminine energy, not unlike most in the quaint church, led me to a section of the parlor that was closed off by a partition wall. Out of nowhere the woman whipped out two crystal daggers, almost like cartoon characters do from their endless pockets.

"These are healing crystal wands," the woman began to explain, noticing my curiosity, "The handles are wrapped in cloth, but beneath the cloth within the crystals are hidden gems. Not gems, literally, but small tokens that the creator felt would aid in the power of these special wands. Water from 42 of the most holy places in the world has been collected and infused into the wands, as have twelve miniscule pictures of holy saints. These wands are most powerful."

The woman continued as I listened intently. Somewhere in the back of my mind I was pondering the price that one of those bad boys went for.

"With the help of these healing crystal wands, I'm going to work to balance your chakras for the next fifteen minutes or so. I will run the wands up, down, and around your energy field and bring you healing and balanced energy to weak chakras. I am only going to focus on the main seven chakras, as well as the earth star chakra located about a foot beneath your feet."

"Once I have balanced your chakras sufficiently, I will ask to bring in the divine feminine. I will also connect you, more than you already are (winks), to the sacred heart of the Universe. How does that sound?"

"It sounds like exactly what I need!" I replied enthusiastically.

She smiled and drew her wands up like she was about to conduct an orchestra.

"Well then, let's begin. I'll let you know when we're done."

The woman went about running the healing crystal wands up, down, and around my energy field. She began at the ground and, within fifteen minutes, worked her way up to my crown chakra. I decided to keep my eyes closed for most of the session, as I immediately felt deeply relaxed as though in a meditative state. I felt content and comfortable and light. When the lady reached my heart chakra, I quickly opened my eyes to see that one of the wands was glowing. Though the wand was what appeared to be clear crystal quartz with no color, I opened my eyes to see it glowing bluish-green. Must have been the reflection of the sunlight coming in through the windows. An illusion.

The woman continued on in her methodical fashion. My eyes were closed once more, but I knew when she reached my crown chakra. The top of my head was tingling excitedly like constant goosebumps. I embraced the feeling and thanked the Universe for this experience of becoming a more balanced and lighter version of myself.

And then I needed to laugh so aggressively. It came on so fast, but I couldn't hold it in. I only giggled at first, but when I opened my eyes and noticed the woman trying to hold in her laugh as well, we both burst out in a fit of laughter.

'I don't! Know why! I'm laughing!" I cried out, trying to catch my breath.

"There sure is a lot of energy up there," the woman giggled.

We laughed for a bit longer while she continued to work on my crown chakra, and then we did a 180. I started crying, again from out of nowhere, as did she. It was as though the woman was poking different parts of my brain, eliciting different human responses with each poke. I didn't feel a central point of sadness, nor did I pinpoint anything funny earlier. I only felt that an intense energy was passing through and causing these physical, human responses. Once we gathered ourselves and cleared the stream of tears running down our faces, the woman spoke again.

"You are a healer. You have healed people, whether you know it or not, and you're going to be a conduit for great healing as time goes on."

Hearing words like that from someone I admired, someone who was doing the same kind of work that I wanted to be involved in for the rest of my life, sent me over the moon. Validation should come from within, but it's always so special to receive validation from outside sources on beliefs, hopes, and dreams. Little hints in this game called life.

The woman continued her work on my chakras, and proceeded to bring in the divine feminine. She called upon numerous feminine powerhouses throughout all of space and time, like Mother Earth, the Egyptian Goddess, Isis, and many more. As she called on each being characterized by sensuality, compassion, peaceful strength, and beyond, I could feel these beings literally standing behind me, divine and complete and unwavering. I felt less alone, and more powerful in a feminine way. I felt like I was being cheered on by these beautiful energies, with their hands on my shoulders and their belief instilled within me. Suffice to say, it was a wonderful feeling that I'd love to metaphorically bottle up and save for later.

And then the woman was complete. She set her healing crystal wands down and smiled at me curiously.

"Sometimes this phenomenon will happen where the wands will connect with your energy so strongly that they'll start glowing different colors-" I cut her off.

"I saw the wands glowing bluish-green!" I yelled out excitedly.

"Precisely! That's exactly what I saw," she exclaimed, "when I reached your heart chakra and began connecting with the energy there, that's when the wands took on the bluish-green glow. Your entire body was actually glowing that color. It was completely enveloping you."

What an absolutely fleeting, fairytale moment.

I left the session smiling too wide. Probably freaked a few people out. This was the kind of place I had been looking for, for so long. A place where I could further my abilities without judgement or misunderstanding, meet like-minded people, and connect with myself and others on a deeper, more supportive and spiritual level. And so I put the weekly Tuesday night development circle into my planner every week as far as the calendar went on, knowing if I didn't write it down that my ADHD would likely win.

When I arrived back at the hostel that same day, I felt a peculiar sensation going on in my back. It only felt tingly at first, then grew into the same feeling as growing pains. Sadly, I've already reached the full extent of my growth. The feeling in my back grew to be more and more annoying as the day progressed, so I knew this had to do with the energy work that had been done on me. Damn you, spiritual expansion and healing! I spent the second half of the day hobbling around, waiting for the next spasm to shoot through my back and incapacitate me.

The next morning was accompanied by even more pain. I forced myself to get out of bed and spend a few hours at a coffee shop crossing homework off of my check list. But when my back pain became so agonizing that I couldn't even entertain the fascinating beliefs of Carl Jung, I decided it would be the perfect time to dip out and head back to the hostel for some meditation. Laying down was sweet relief. I found it easier than normal to drowsily succumb to peaceful mindfulness. I meditated for three hours, which became a high score in my personal experience.

My meditation was slightly interrupted three times by outside noises that are constantly happening at the busy hostel. On the third meditation, I switched from binaural beats to a guided meditation meant for contacting spirit guides. I felt so deeply relaxed that I thought my vibration could be high, and the contact could come with ease. Shortly into the guided meditation, I found myself in a dream it seemed, though I was partially aware of my existence and my surroundings. Partially not. This was a random dream in the midst of everything I was experiencing in the present moment, but I like the message it provided. I was walking through a crowd of partying kids, when I saw these two massive, intimidating guys. They were heavily decked out in black attire, looking hardcore with piercings and eyeliner and chains. Everyone else was steering clear of them, but I felt pulled in their direction.

"Hello!" I smiled goofily at them, hoping to break the very chilly ice.

They didn't say anything at first, but just continued staring daggers into my soul. In awkward retaliation, I did this jig that I do when I feel uncomfortable. It makes everyone else feel a little uncomfortable too. The big beefy guys started laughing. With me, not at me.

"Morgan! Everyone else is afraid of us, but not you," one of the two chuckled.

The other continued, "we're not mean or scary, we're just perceived that way."

"Oh I know, I see right through you," I teased, already bumping elbows with the two.

It was a quick dream/meditation, but that particular theme stumbles across my dream state often. I am presented with what appears to be darkness, and I come to realize by experience or intuition that darkness is not singularly synonymous with evil or bad. We have come to perceive it that way. We all have both darkness and light in this duality based, 3-dimensional physical world. It is not something to be feared, but brought to awareness and handled with love and non-judgement. I think these two, whether real beings or creations by my subconscious, came to me to reinforce that important notion. I hope to see them again.

The back pain subsided a few days later. God *is* merciful! I think I convinced a few curious people to explore energy work as a result of my curious back pain. I think some thought I was crazy, but c'est la vie!

My time at the hostel rolled on. After a fast-paced week of doing all things free with guests in the Phoenix area, my introversion was forcing me to shut down. So I holed up inside my bedroom at the hostel and used the downtime to watch youtube videos on the many different perspectives that the broadness of spirituality encompasses. I was pulled to watch a video titled *The Four Levels of Consciousness,* as my ego loves to put myself into levels, categories, and boxes. The first level of consciousness explained in the video was characterized by feeling as though the world is happening *to* you, whereas the fourth was total enlightenment, knowing that a world exists inside of you. I was trying to determine where exactly I would fit into the four levels, over-analyzing my own awareness. A woman began to talk on the topic of intuition, explaining that it's one of our best abilities as humans, yet we don't utilize it enough. We throw it to the wayside, in disbelief that we could have such innate power and understanding over things that aren't crystal clear before us in the physical world. This woman went on to talk about the disconnect between intuition and the critical mind. The critical mind screams whereas intuition whispers, so naturally it's difficult to hear intuition unless we strengthen it.

Backtrack to Sedona real quick. My momma and I each received auric field images. With your hand pressed to a sensor, the aura imaging machine picks up on your electromagnetic field. Radio waves are sent out by the machine and through the sensors that your hand rests on. The radio waves interact with your electromagnetic field, and are converted into electrical energy which allows for the processing of light and color. AKA, your aura. Not only did I see my aura, but I was given a hefty, hole-punched report on different characteristics and experiences that I'm privy to based off of my colors; aspects of myself that I eventually overanalyzed, as is my tendency, stated in the report. My point is, one of the details in the report explained that my mind governs my life considerably more than my body or my spirit. My mind encompassed about 60% of control, whereas my body and spirit each made up about 20%. Disappointing, but not surprising. I am on a journey back to spirit.

So when I was watching this video on consciousness, hearing about the battle between the critical mind and intuition, I was well aware of my own critical mind's tendency to scream over my humble intuition. I smacked the space button on my laptop, pausing the video. I asked myself, at this moment, without putting any thought into it, what is your intuition whispering?

Write your book, I heard thoughtlessly.

That wasn't what I expected, but I accepted it. I was not going to allow my critical mind to overanalyze. It'd been a crazy few weeks getting acquainted at the hostel and the last thing on my mind was working on my book. But I wasn't going to overanalyze what I heard. I hadn't worked on my book in weeks. Months, really. But *no overanalyzing*!

I unpaused the video. The woman continued.

"Your intuition says, 'write that book, call that guy, start that company…"

I paused the video again. Did I hear it correctly? Was the first example that the woman gave of the whispering intuition to *write. that. book*? What a weird, weird coincidence, am I right? Or maybe, what an incredible form of validation. I'll go with the latter. Suffice to say, I spent the entire next day hidden in the dark corner of a coffee shop with a dark-roast coffee glued to my hand, ideas flowing onto paper. Did you know that when you're doing what makes you completely and genuinely happy, you are connecting with your highest and purest self?

As I acclimated further into living at the hostel, and in Arizona in general, I discovered how powerful meditation was. Not discovered, really, but remembered. When I'd get all sweaty and overwhelmed and practically mute from the overuse of my already limited supply of extraversion, I was led to meditation. And so it became the most important part of my daily routine, as it should be. After the first day of a twenty minute meditation session in my teeny bedroom, I felt peaceful, albeit sleepy. After the second consecutive day, I felt refreshed. And on the third day, invigorated. Each time I meditated, I quickly fell into a state that teetered between conscious awareness and deep, subconscious exploration that sometimes felt like I was sleeping for two minutes and then brought back to awareness by a random idea or vivid image flitting by. During one of my meditations, the likes of which usually lasted thirty minutes, I heard a very clear voice. There are times when I question if I created voices or images with my highly creative right-brain, as well as instances when I know how clearly and definitely I did *not* create something. And this was one of those clear instances of the voice *definitely* not being my creation.

    I heard, "We're not coming *your* way, Morgan."

    That statement, so purposeful and bold. My ego, so wounded.

    I plucked the headphones from my ears, eyes popping open after hearing this declaration. I deduced that my highest and purest soul team, my loved ones and guides, were making it clear that they would not be lowering their vibrations any further to reach me. I would have to put in the work to reach them. I would have to continue to raise my vibration and expand in ways that resulted from spiritual discipline.

    That was another lightbulb moment in the continual illumination of my spiritual expansion. I knew that I was capable of pushing past my self-imposed boundaries to continue advancing my frequency, and the Universe knew as well. Now it's just a matter of continuing to take inspired action, with discipline as the backbone, to actively make it happen. Basically the Universe was pulling a dad move. Got it, I need to put in the work; practice. Classic.

    I continued using meditation as the proper tool for combatting the physical world around me and the overly analytical thoughts inside of me. I also used meditation to justify taking naps, because my meditations *always* led to naps. I know this, but I pretend I don't and simply let nature take its course. As I continued on and constantly deepened my meditative experiences, I learned something vital to my personal meditation expansion that I think is important to share. At the spiritualist church, I overheard a group of women conversing about meditation techniques. Imagine me hiding behind a wall with my head popping out just enough to listen in. I heard the term *monkey thoughts*. These are random, annoying thoughts that pop in your head when you're attempting to clear your mind during meditation. Thoughts that come from nowhere, and that won't easily disappear. You envision yourself on a train, and see the thoughts flying out the window, but alas they catch back up and hitch a ride.

In my past experiences, I have always tried to take those thoughts and collectively toss them into a burlap sack. Dispose of the sack. Try to ignore these ideas entirely, giving them no time or day because they weren't important. And that's where I went wrong. These thoughts are the first to pop in our minds for a reason. They take up space, whether consciously or subconsciously. They take up our energy. It's important for the process of achieving mindfulness to give these thoughts the time and energy they deserve. We can focus our attention on them for a short or long duration. However long it takes to see them fully, and, eventually, fully accept letting them go. It's incredible really how easy this makes relaxing your mind. Flow with what comes instead of arguing or denying. Mindfulness isn't a race, but a dance. The monkey thoughts will leave when they're ready. So from here on out, we acknowledge. We no longer repress or dismiss or subdue with mechanisms of the egotistical, critical mind. We face the monkey thoughts. We empathize with the monkey thoughts. And then we release the monkey thoughts back into the wild unknown where they belong. As the thoughts continue to pop in, be addressed with compassion, and be released with awareness, a deeper state of relaxation becomes not just possible but easy.

*   *   *   *   *

Time marched on in a linear fashion, as it does on this physical plane, and I continued my typical way of life at the hostel. Everyday was a new adventure. I'd rise early, seeing as though it was nearly impossible to sleep in with the constant movement of people and energy. The smell of coffee wafting from the kitchen would pull me from my sleepy stupor. I'd amble out onto the porch from my bedroom, and breathe in the beautiful Arizona mornings everyday. And when I say everyday, I mean every single day. Each morning is characterized by bright, cloudless skies. A fresh start every cycle of 24 hours. The only downside is that I never had an excuse to stay inside with the curtains drawn and binge watch Netflix indie and scary movies. I had this annoying, motivated urge to be productive and active. Curse you, Arizona, and your beautiful, uncompromising weather. Oh yes, the coffee. The smell of freshly brewed grounds would pull me from my passing interaction with the morning sun and the birds, into the common area to meet the new people who had checked into the hostel the previous night. Each morning was like Christmas, and the people were shiny new toys. I was delighted to fill my coffee cup and greet all the new souls I had the privilege of coming into contact with, if only for an ephemeral moment in this particular space and time. I was antsy, from the coffee and my own curiosity, to hear of their travels, learn their stories, and come closer to understanding another one of the infinite perspectives that minutely and eternally makes up the Universe. It was a blessing to be humbled by these people who were coming and going. I constantly found myself thinking of how brilliant and how curious it was that I had the privilege of crossing paths with all of those souls at the divine time that I did. How brilliant and curious that they might impart some new perspective on me in the midst of my intentional spiritual journey. I felt simultaneously humbled down and renewed in my passion for experiencing life. Send all of the spiritual catalysts my way! Rejoiced the introvert. But crossing paths with souls that impart knowledge on you is a common theme, whether you acknowledge it or not. Whether you live in a hostel or not. I had been holding this awareness for years, and it seemed that my move to Arizona turned the meet-and-greets to overdrive.

  I crossed paths with all kinds of people, with all kinds of knowledge to share. I paid careful attention to the information I was presented with, like a good student is apt to do. A lot of the time, the information I happened upon led me down a rabbithole of more research. This is the case for the topic of astrology, which I'm still trying to wrap my head around. There's a lot to it, if you didn't know. At the spiritualist church, I met a girl who knew astrology forwards and backwards; who imparted the desire to explore astrology further onto me. Before exchanging names, she questioned, "Are you a Sag?"

  "You betcha," I replied enthusiastically, accidentally giving my midwestern identity away.

  And she was a Pisces. It was pretty much stamped on her forehead, considering the empathetic and creative nature she so obviously exhibited; the intuitive energy she exuded.

  "My mom's a Sagittarius!" she exclaimed, directing me to her momma standing in the corner.

  I thought for a moment, "Wait! My mom's a *Pisces!*"

  "That tends to happen," she continued, "it's more common than you'd think."

She went on to explain that the dynamic between a Pisces and a Sagittarius is an expansive one. The feminine water sign, Pisces, and the masculine fire sign, Sagittarius, complement each other. Water signs crave security, whereas fire signs crave freedom. These signs can learn a great deal about contrast from each other. I applied this newfound knowledge to the relationship between my momma and me. I help my momma to embrace the unknown; to expand her horizons both spiritually and physically. My momma inspires me with her divine feminine energy; a particular energy that simultaneously flows and works hard.

The next time the girl from the spiritualist church and I crossed paths, neither of us could remember the other's name.

"Sagittarius!" she shouted my way.

"Pisces!" I waved back.

The spiritualist church quickly became my favorite spot in Phoenix. And there are many, many great spots. The church had a way of making me feel understood, part of a whole, inspired, and limitless. I've never been a church kinda girl, but Rising Phoenix Spiritualist Church made me want to stay in on Saturday nights so I could be fresh and lively for the Sunday healing services.

The spiritualist church had a jam-packed calendar full of classes, healing sessions, and special guest appearances by new and known members of the spiritualist community. On a slow night at the hostel, three of us, Benny, Molly, and I, decided to investigate a free *all messages* night. A local psychic-medium would be offering messages to whomever she felt compelled from 7-9pm. We stepped into the common area where about twenty chairs were set up in a circular fashion. Not knowing exactly what to expect, but excited at the possibilities, we eagerly took our seats. The night began by each person in the room picking a tarot card from a basket. These were no ordinary tarot cards. They were original cat-themed cards. Very wholesome, in my opinion. When the basket was presented before me, I reached in with the intention of openness and receptivity, knowing that I would absolutely pick the card that was intended for me. The Universe would have it no other way.

I pulled a card.

The Fool.

My favorite card! The card that had been appearing way too frequently in my readings recently to be coincidental that night. Not that I believe in coincidences anyway. It was the card that I most resonated with at the moment in the tarot. The card that represents walking excitedly into the unknown. The card in the deck labeled 0, meaning clean slate, infinite potential, childlike wonder.

"Ahh the Fool," the woman whispered, staring at me with a blank face for a moment, "my *favorite!*" she squealed.

"Mine too!" I answered excitedly.

"So you're working on your passions," she questioned slightly, though she knew the answer.

"I have many things in the works right now," I replied coyly.

"Yes you do. Keep going. You have the Universe on your side," and with that, she moved onto one of my friends that tagged along.

After offering her interpretation of the cards that we three picked, the woman addressed us three as a collective.

"You girls came together, yes?" she inquired.

We nodded simultaneously.

"You girls have a very strong connection. You're friends, but do you work together?" she asked us.

We all nodded again.

Molly, the hostel's operations manager, spoke up, "We all volunteer at the hostel in downtown Phoenix."

The woman nodded, "Ahh, I see. And you are each so different, but you complement one another."

We looked at each other, and nodded, understanding entirely what she meant. Molly, with beautiful red hair, emanated peace-power and activism. Benny, from Brazil, bold and spunky, unapologetically herself and hardworking. And me, blonde at the moment, curious and observant, a student always, with my spirituality leading the way. Each of us, powerful in our own right and with an energy so entirely our own.

"You three coming together at the hostel was not by accident. On the contrary, the Universe made it happen for a reason. I feel as though you three shared past lifetimes together. You seem too connected for just this one lifetime," the woman explained.

She continued on, "I see you three as witches."

Molly, Benny, and I shared excited looks, smirking contentedly. Being referred to as a witch was nothing new to me, though I don't consider myself a witch… in this lifetime. Still, it made me feel recognized for my divine power. The term feels synonymous with goddess. Or badass.

When the event concluded, we three left the little church on Encanto Avenue with a newfound connection. Little did the woman know that a week prior, us girls at the hostel held our first full moon ritual. We cleansed ourselves with the proper smudging tools in dramatic fashion. We crafted lists personal to each of us, outlining all the physical and non-physical energies that we were leaving behind with the cycle of the moon. Things that were no longer serving us or aiding us in our highest and purest purpose. We burned our lists and allowed the ashes and energy to make their way back to Mother Earth, to be purified and reimagined. The corner of my list caught the match's flame with ease, but Benny struggled in this endeavor for some mystical, energetic reason. We watched on as Benny battled to get the paper to start on fire, first working at the corners with the small flame and then placing the paper on the ground and dropping match after match upon it. We collectively had to help her burn the list that obviously she held a great deal of attachment to. Spooky. We took turns picking tarot and oracle cards, sharing when we particularly resonated with the messages. And it seemed that we all resonated with our messages that night, whether we liked it or not as is the way of the tarot.

So at that intimate gathering at the Rising Phoenix Spiritualist Church, we were honored to be referred to as witches. When I reflect on it, I realize how synonymously our way of creating reality is likened to witchcraft. Our words, thoughts, and energies are spells that with the right intentions can so effortlessly shift reality. A dash of surrender, a sprinkle of gratitude, a dump-truck load of unconditional love, and *ta-da*! Visions coming to fruition. The best part is we all have access to the spells, and there are plenty of ingredients to go around.

As it goes, the full moon was soon enough followed by a new moon. And thus, a new moon ritual. Us girls at the hostel decided to make it a recurring ritual considering how divinely powerful and reenergized the full moon experience had us feeling. At the peak of the new moon, we took on a similar, but opposite approach. We saged ourselves, clearing all negative attachments and heavy energies. We crafted lists personal to each of us, detailing all the physical and non-physical energies we wanted to bring into our lives. Energies that would assist us in our individual highest and purest purposes. We spoke affirmations out loud around a weak fire, but a fire that stayed aflame nonetheless. We pulled tarot and oracle cards that once again left us feeling understood, connected, and maybe a little bit attacked. We nibbled on hors d'oeuvres until someone suggested pizza, because manifesting makes you hangry. And when our hunger was satisfied, we danced. Us girls, fed by cheese pizza, and the fire, fed by the pizza box and paper plates. The energy was euphoric and light and powerful all rolled into one sensation. I laughed with childlike innocence, and sweated equally as much. There's no way I hadn't done a similar ritual in a past life. It felt familiar to dance around the fire like a lunatic, embodying the flames with my crazed steps. The movement meant freedom, the fire meant power, and the new moon offered us a fresh beginning to decide how we wanted to act on those concepts.

When the next Sunday healing service at the church rolled around, us three girls decided to make a stop again. In syncopated steps, we glided down the block en route. Naturally, someone tried to take our power by cat-calling us from a car window.

"We'll put a *hex* on you!" Molly shouted back, not missing a beat.

This time, I signed up for straight-up energy healing. I had just enough time to make a round at the snack table before being called to my session. The lady offering the healing explained the process to me. I was familiar with it, having already experienced Reiki from my momma and a few other powerful energy healers back in Wisconsin. She would be running her hands up and down through my energy field, scanning my body but never putting her hands on me. She'd be able to pick up on imbalances in my chakras, and anything perceived as negative in my physical and spiritual bodies. I sat patiently in my chair, breathing deeply to enter a meditative state in hopes that her work would be easier. The woman began to breathe deeply as well, pulling in clean energy from the Universe to replace any stagnant, heavy energy that was attached to me. Energy healing involves clearing old, weak energy out. The lady did this visually by mimicking a gesture of pulling gunk out of my body. She'd find a weak area, pull the invisible gunk out of my energy vortexes, and then blow the air quickly to make the negative energy disperse. This process went on for a few minutes. I could feel it actively working; a shift occurring. Each pull of gunk from my spiritual body reaffirmed my belief in the power of energy healing by a delayed onslaught of goosebumps on the crown of my head. It wasn't a single time, or a few instances. The attack of goosebumps on the top of my head continued again and again at the same time over and over - a moment after the woman would blow the air to break up the energy. This cycle continued until the lady plopped into her chair and rested. My body was tingling, and noticeably lighter than a few minutes prior.

"I'm not quite finished, but I have a bunch of messages that I should start delivering to you before I forget what they are," she explained, chuckling to herself.

She began relaying what was pertinent to share with me.

"You believe you have a problem with your throat chakra, correct? That is not so. There is a disconnect between your solar plexus chakra and your heart chakra. The solar plexus is the energy center associated with self-worth. The heart, love. Due to this disconnect, your throat chakra is slightly imbalanced. But once you foster that relationship between your solar plexus and heart, your throat chakra will be wonderful."

My jaw was likely on the floor. My throat chakra was probably shaking it's metaphorical head at me, knowingly. Since I could remember, I had been blaming my weak throat chakra singularly. What the woman explained made sense when I reflected on it later. A disconnect between identity and love? Self-love and self-acceptance are easy to preach, but not always to practice. Our egos make that so. My ego *loved* to make that so.

"There's more," the woman continued, "I see your higher self. Right behind you. Right behind your head and a little further above. She's very, very clear to me. Usually when I do this work I can sense others' higher selves, but I rarely see them. And yours is right there. Very prominent."

I whipped around, thinking maybe I could catch a glimpse.

"Do you understand what your higher self is?" the lady asked before continuing further. Your higher self is the most enlightened and purest form of your soul, not infected by physical reality prejudices, judgements, attachments, or beliefs. Your higher self sees and knows, through all directions and dimensions of space and time, as though perched high up in the sky with a most opportune vantage point to guide you on your physical journey. Your higher self is within reach, for each and every one of us. It's simply a matter of wanting that connection and raising your vibration to make it happen.

"Your higher self is trying so hard to make contact, but it's your analytical mind that is preventing that connection. I would like to help you connect with your higher self right now, if you're interested in establishing that connection."

Is this what networking is like? Making connections with more powerful and influential people to help pave the way to new and exciting opportunities? I giddily agreed, grateful that I was being assisted by such a divinely powerful woman in my quest for spiritual expansion. And this seemed like a peak moment thus far on my journey.

The woman stood and began motioning my higher self forward with closed eyes and slow, methodical movements. Going into the Sunday healing service that day, I had a lot on my mind per usual. How long did I want to commit to volunteering at the hostel? When should I buy a plane ticket home for the holidays? Should I even go home for the holidays? Should I start looking at apartments already? Do I have enough money to get by? The woman guided me to stand, and by motioning with her hands and verbally calling to my higher self, she coaxed my physical mind and the higher energy into connecting. So although I had all of these questions and more fighting for a chance at the podium in my head, they were suddenly quieted. Still existing, but suddenly with less pressure. While only seconds before they were sending my mind into a frenzy, they now held a neutrality that didn't affect me. In that space came a sense of peace of mind that was so foreign to my physical experience. A peace that was the result of remembering a fraction of the feeling of connection to source. It wasn't as though I spontaneously had the answers to all of my questions, but I had the relief that accompanies remembering my true beingness. I am in the hands of the Universe, divinely guided, just as I am the very hands that shape the stars, the moons, and all of the suns. Everything was working out exactly the way it was supposed to. The perfect unfolding of experiences for my soul's continued expansion. And so these questions that my ego held onto so tightly seemed so trivial in this moment of connection with my higher self.

"Did you feel that?" the woman questioned, as my ego's metaphorical walls were being demolished by bombs of truth and love and light.

"Yup," I eloquently replied between shockwaves.

The lady instructed me to call on my higher self when I needed guidance. And if I know myself, I'll be there when called on. Unless my highest and purest self was taking a nap, then I might have to be patient.

The woman had more to share with me yet.

"I saw you as a pioneer woman in a past life."

So earlier when I said connecting with my higher self was peaking, I lied. Learning that I was a pioneer woman traversing the Oregon Trail was undoubtedly the highlight of my life thus far.

"Oh wow! That's the coolest thing I've ever heard. But why did that visual come through? Why is it important for me to know at this moment?"

Gimme the details! I live for past lives.

"You aren't from Arizona, are you?" she inquired. I shook my head no.

"Ahh so there's that obvious parallel from that past life and this current lifetime. You traveled great distances in both lifetimes in search of something better. But beyond that, there is a deeper reason that the vision came to me. You have a deep, deep strength in your soul that you may not have recognized yet in this lifetime. But it's there. You are strong, and your soul remembers that. You have the power and determination and strength to accomplish what your soul needs to accomplish. You did it in that past lifetime, and you'll do the same in this lifetime. It's just who you are"

It was funny hearing that particular message of strength, as a mantra had popped into my head only a few days prior. Simple and to the point: *I am strong*. I felt around that time that I needed the support that affirmations can so easily provide. In that message of my past life as a pioneer woman, the woman provided me with the understanding that I could channel the strength I needed from inside of me, as I've carried it lifetime to lifetime. I carry it with me always, like my backpack slung over my shoulder.

"What do you want to do in life?" the woman questioned, "Do you want to work in this kind of field? Something with spirituality?"

After years of dreading being asked this question by those who couldn't relate with me, I felt an unfamiliar sense of excitement and freedom answering authentically.

"Yes," I spoke quietly at first and then faster and faster, "it's the thing that makes me feel fulfilled and inspired and purposeful and passionate. I want to learn endlessly, and I want to share what I know because my life hasn't been the same, in the best way possible, since I tapped into what I have."

"Good," the woman replied smiling back at me, "that's what you are here to do. You're on exactly the right path. Regardless of what others say or believe in regard to your path. Does that resonate?"

It did.

"You know your path. You know it deep down, and your higher self will continue to guide you with feelings of excitement and passion. Remember that your path is perfect for you. It will unfold exactly how it is supposed to. Does what I'm saying resonate?"

"Completely," I affirmed, a noticeable twinkle in my eye I'm sure.

The woman continued on.

"Keep doing what you're doing. You are in *exactly* the right place for right now. The valley. Arizona. It's no surprise that you ended up here," the woman stated like she knew how the story ended. But I didn't need the ending spoiled. In that moment, I was content romanticizing the up in the air unfolding of all that was to come. The greatest stories are the ones that have you completely unsure of what will happen next, and that was how I experienced my spiritual journey so far. In the short month I had been in Arizona, I had expanded far beyond what I thought I was capable of spiritually. I mean, hey! Somewhere along the way I even started sleeping without a light or a TV on. Chapter 2 Morgan could never. But the real, soulful expansion was characterized by deep understandings that I uncovered from both outside and within me. From meditation, signs, and spiritual catalysts whose paths I crossed. Such as the power of manifestation, the Law of Attraction, eternal life, unconditional love, and the notion of endless learning. I was called to follow my heart in this lifetime, like every great protagonist. I was called to expand spiritually. I was called to be curious, constantly. I was called to Arizona. And because I listened, the Universe continues to call. I pick up everytime... almost every time. I'm human.

*   *   *   *   *

The experiences I had from the very beginning to the present moment in time and space have been paramount in shaping the foundation of my spiritual expansion.

Obviously I learned a great deal in the expanse of time that this chronology details. But I'm not naive enough to think that my education is complete. Far from it. I've always loved the notion of being a student, and I think that will be so until I depart. There are simply too many books to be read and beings to connect with to *not* be a student, always. These first experiences and indoctrinations into my spiritual expansion were crucial. Looking back, I realize how divinely concocted the journey has been. From the anecdotes recorded in my journals, to the inspirations in the form of beautiful beings and fleeting signs, to the endlessly supportive spiritual catalysts and teachers that seemed to offer me teachings at exactly the right time everytime. What a beautiful dance of highs and lows, all working for my highest and purest purpose whether evident or hidden in between the lines.

Through sharing this, I hope you feel inspired to explore as I have. To question the constructs that are being outgrown. I hope you feel inspired to open up to your personal spiritual journey of expansion. I hope you find comfort in writing your experiences down and connecting the puzzle pieces that are laying scattered, waiting to be put back together. Piece by piece, the image becomes clearer.

I feel I've tapped into a most glorious form of magic that only needs to be remembered for each of us to wield it. Let's use our powers for good and spread messages of the reality of manifesting, the understanding of eternal life, the power of love, and beyond. Because, as a student is inclined to do, we'll keep unearthing more and more information about love and light that would do well to be shared.

I pride myself on the journey I've faced thus far. It's too soon to tell where I'm going, but with the organization of my experiences laid out before me, at least I know where I've been. Sometimes I rode the bus, other times I drove, but I ended up at this point and I'm determined to continue on. The destination is always changing, but right now in my head it looks something like being able to control my developing abilities with at least a bit of grace. Or maybe it looks like the wish I made on Jean Anne's tarot card all those years ago coming true. Whatever the case, you'll find me somewhere along my unique and perfect spiritual journey with curiosity leading the way...

Writing all of my experiences down.

www.ingramcontent.com/pod-product-compliance
Lightning Source LLC
Chambersburg PA
CBHW050112170426
43198CB00014B/2548